FOR ORGANS, PIANOS & ELECTRONIC KEYBOARDS

E-Z PLAY TODAY
120

The Gospel Songs
of
Bill and Gloria Gaither

T0048387

ISBN 978-0-7935-0544-9

HAL•LEONARD®
CORPORATION
7777 W. BLUEMOUND RD. P.O. BOX 13819 MILWAUKEE, WI 53213

Abide In Me

Registration 3
Rhythm: Waltz

Words by Gloria Gaither
Music by William J. Gaither and Chris Christian

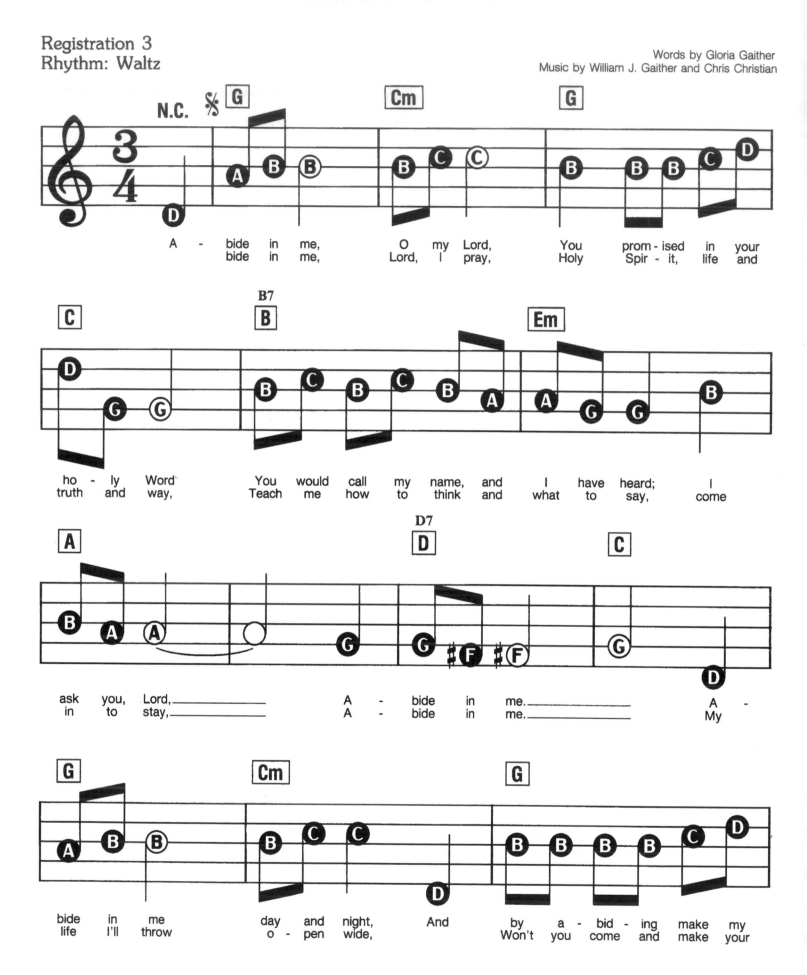

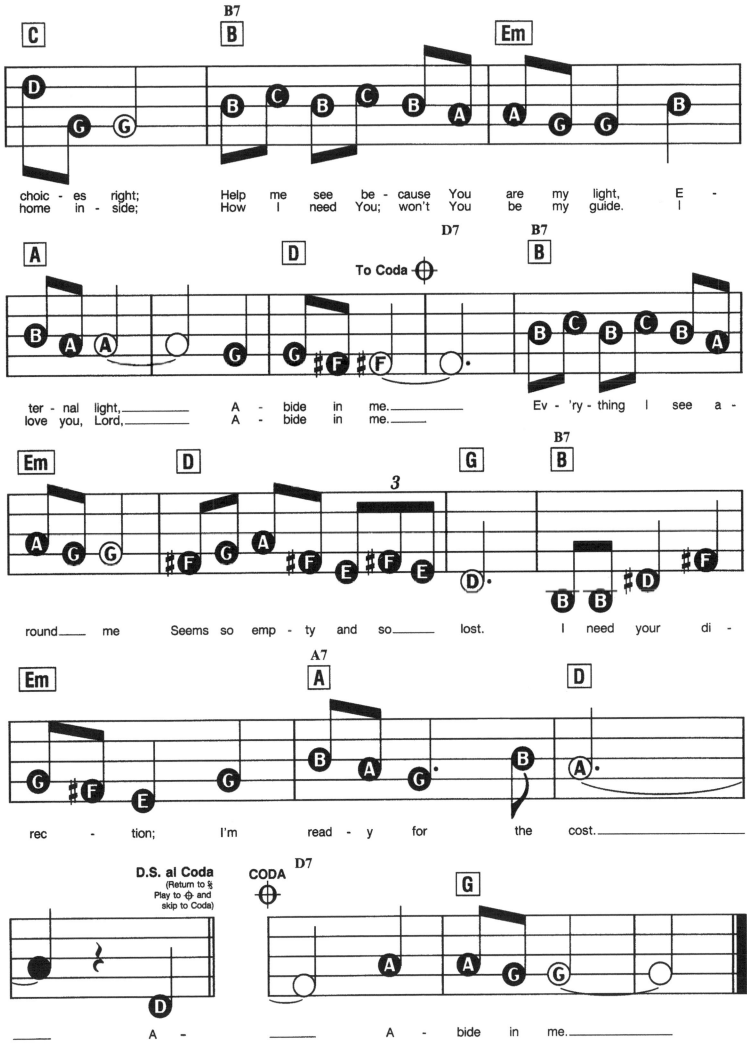

All God's Children

Registration 4

Words by Charles Milhuff and William J. Gaither
Music by William J. Gaither

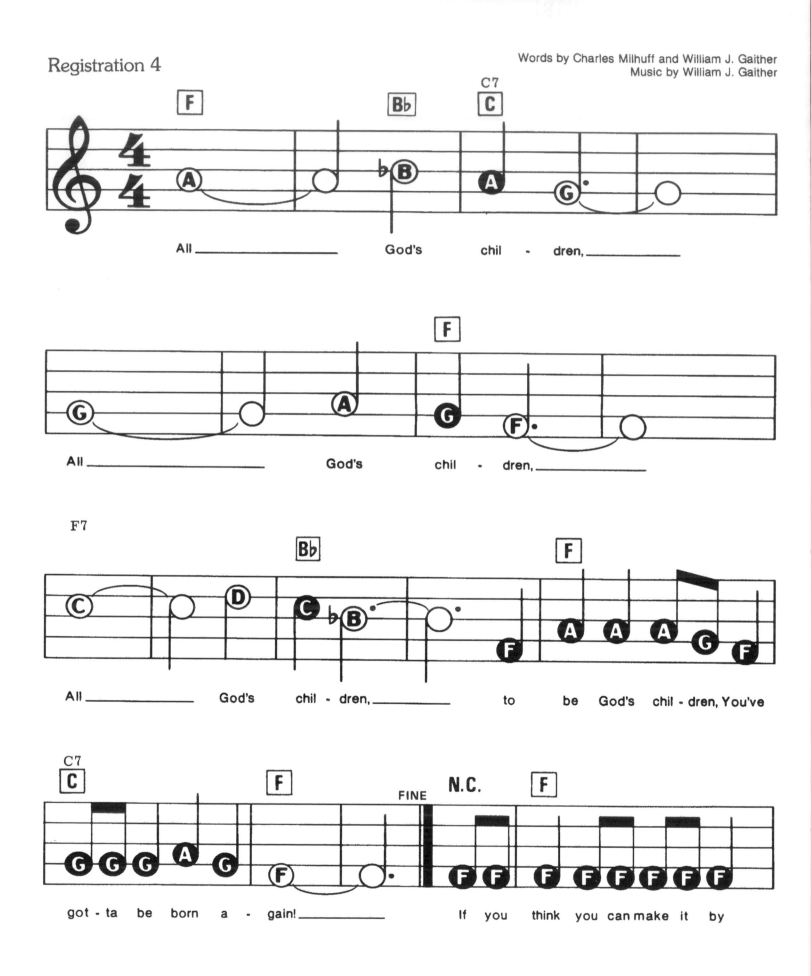

go - 'in to church, then you're just kid - din' your - self. If you

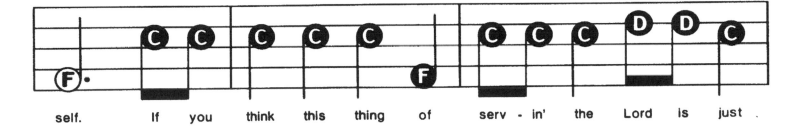

think you can make it by do - in' good works, then you're just kid - din' your -

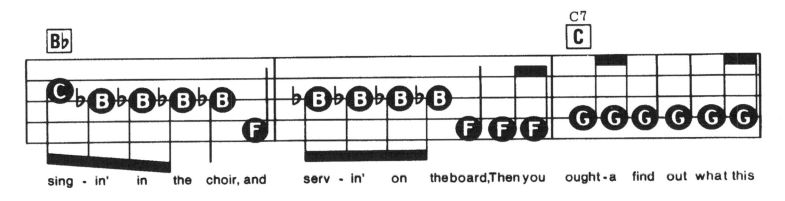

self. If you think this thing of serv - in' the Lord is just

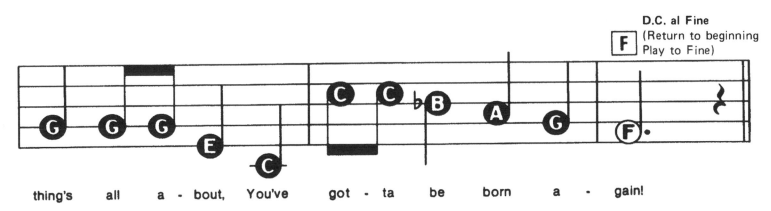

sing - in' in the choir, and serv - in' on the board, Then you ought - a find out what this

D.C. al Fine
(Return to beginning
Play to Fine)

thing's all a - bout, You've got - ta be born a - gain!

At The Foot Of The Cross

Registration 6
Rhythm: Waltz

Words by W. Dale Oldham
Music by William J. Gaither

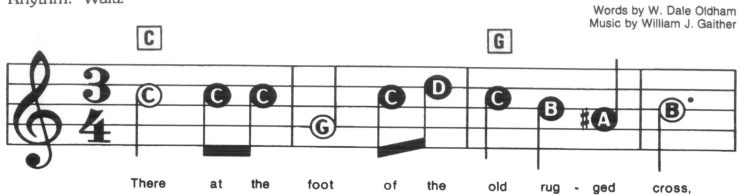

There at the foot of the old rug - ged cross,

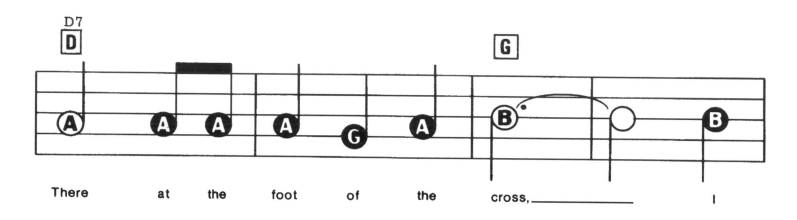

There at the foot of the cross,_____ I

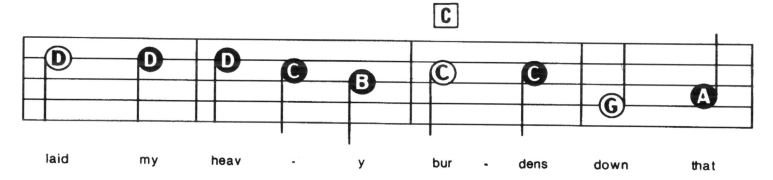

laid my heav - y bur - dens down that

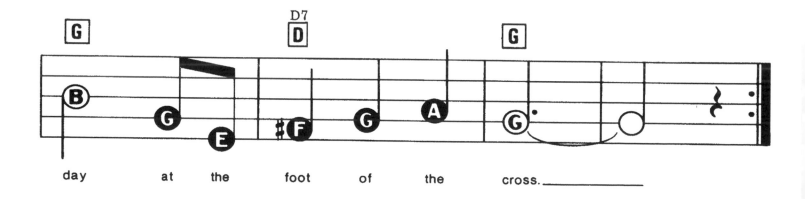

day at the foot of the cross._____

Created In His Image

Registration 6
Rhythm: Waltz

Words by William J. & Gloria Gaither
and Dorothy Sickal
Music by William J. Gaither

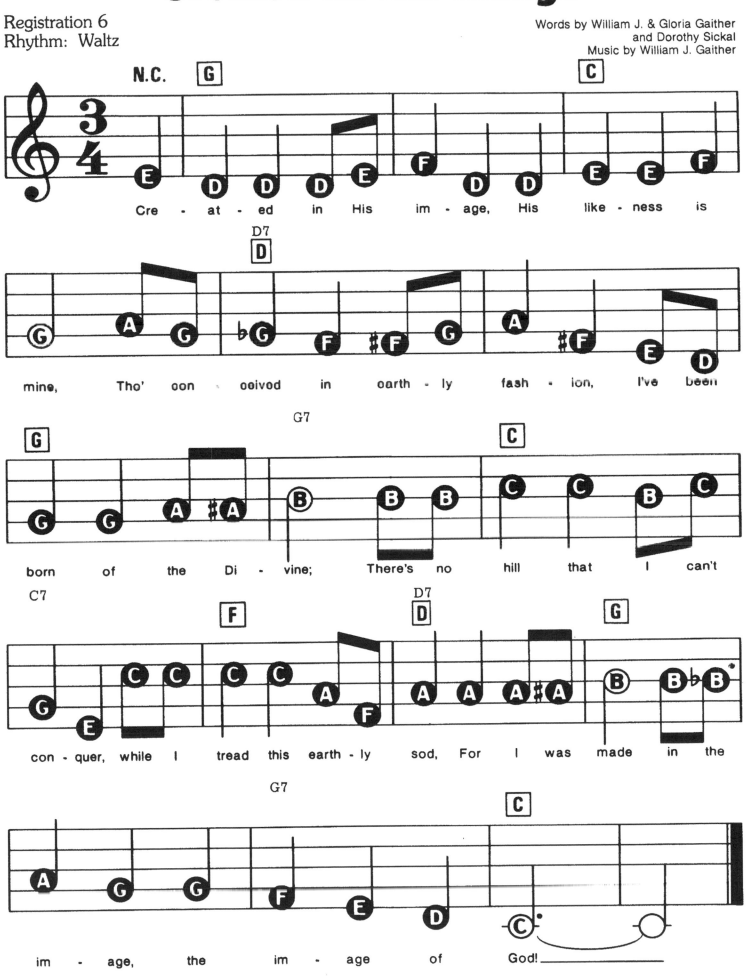

Because He Lives

Registration 2
Rhythm: Fox Trot or Swing

Words by William J. & Gloria Gaither
Music by William J. Gaither

God sent His Son, _____ they called Him
day _____ I'll cross Him that

Je - sus; _____ He came to love, _____ heal and for -
ri - ver; _____ I'll fight life's fi - nal war with

give; _____ He lived and died _____ to buy my
pain; _____ And then as death _____ gives way to

par - don, _____ An emp - ty grave is there to prove my Sav - ior
vic - t'ry, _____ I'll see the lights of glo - ry and I'll know He

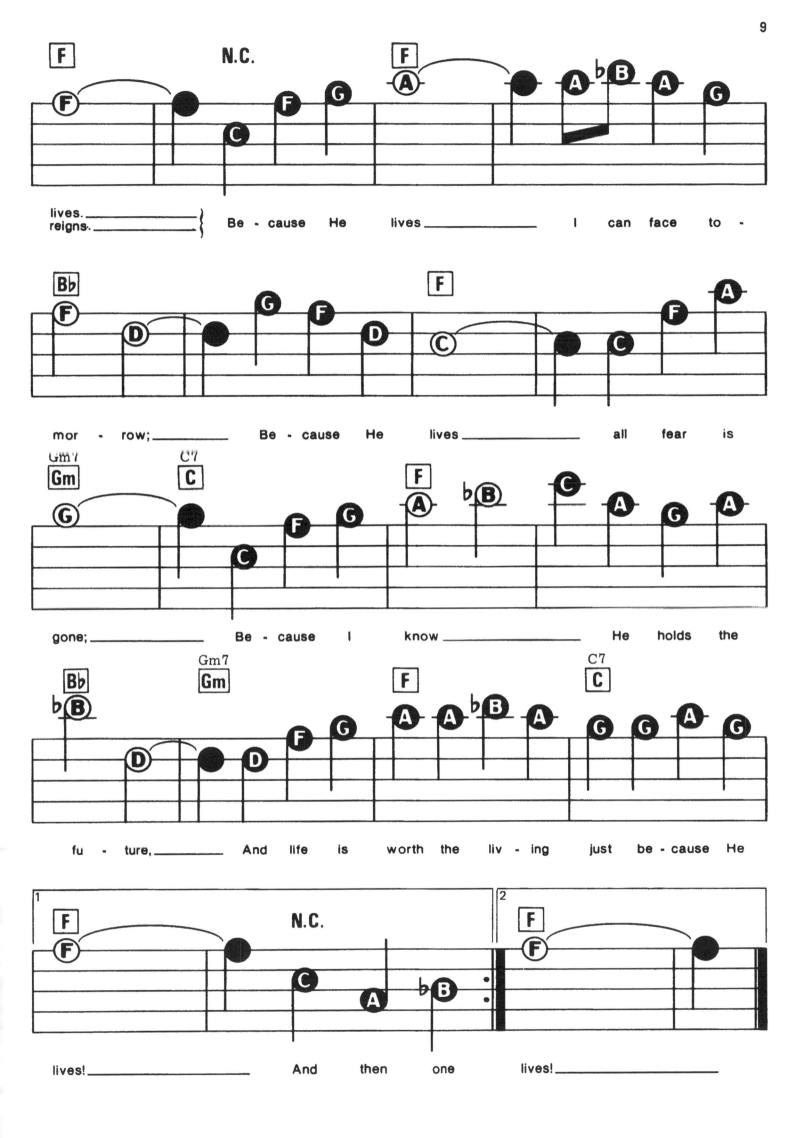

Broken And Spilled Out

Registration 3
Rhythm: Waltz

Words by Gloria Gaither
Music by Bill George

Calm Assurance

Registration 5
Rhythm: Fox Trot or Swing

Words by William J. and Gloria Gaither
Music by William J. Gaither

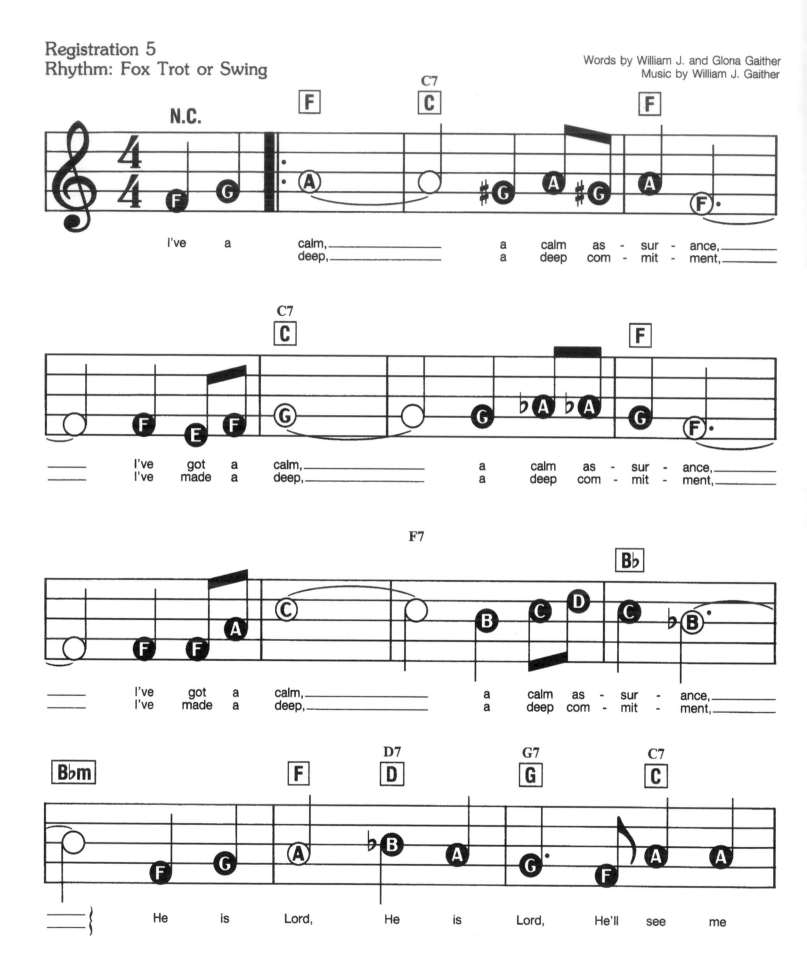

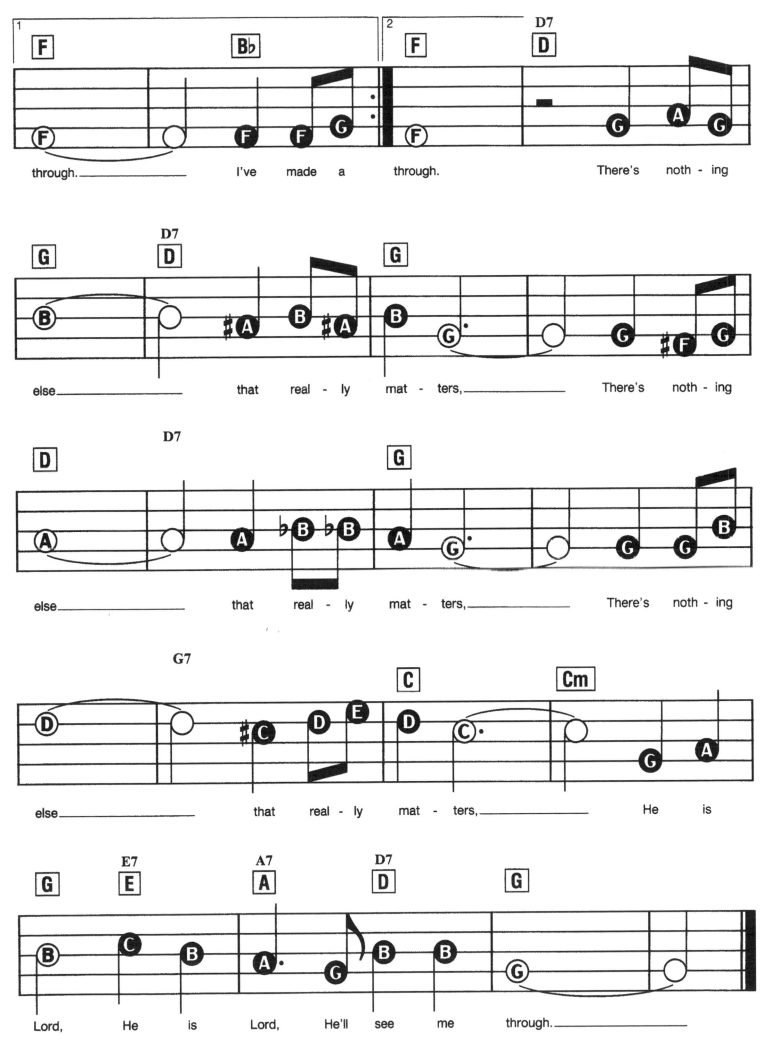

The Church Triumphant

Registration 6
Rhythm: Waltz

Words and Music by
William J. & Gloria Gaither

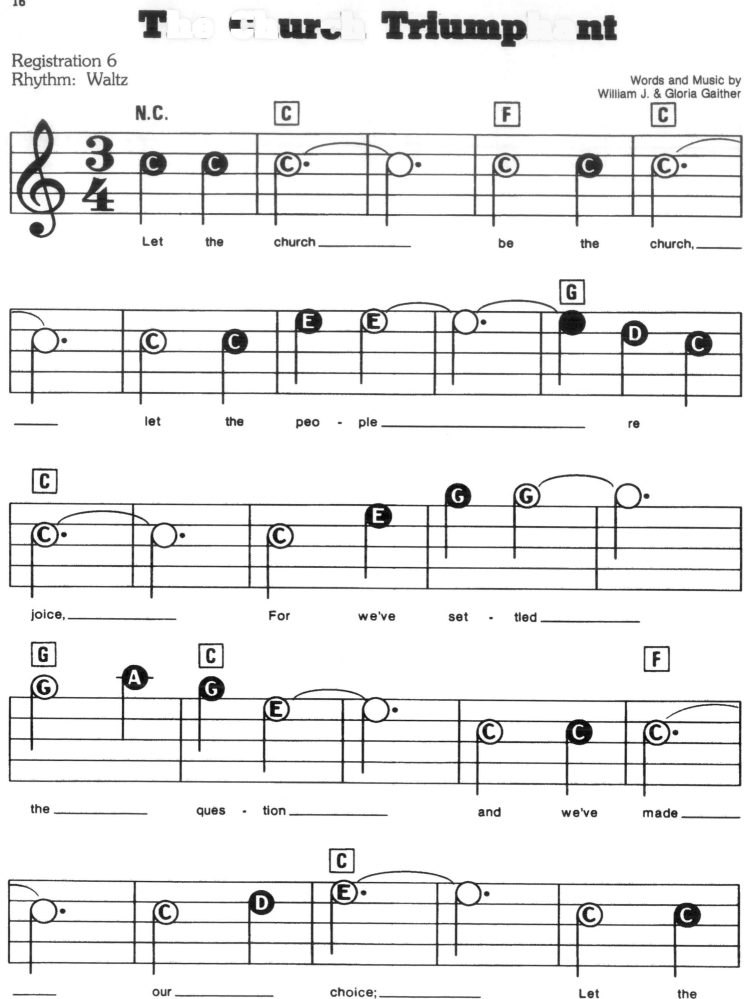

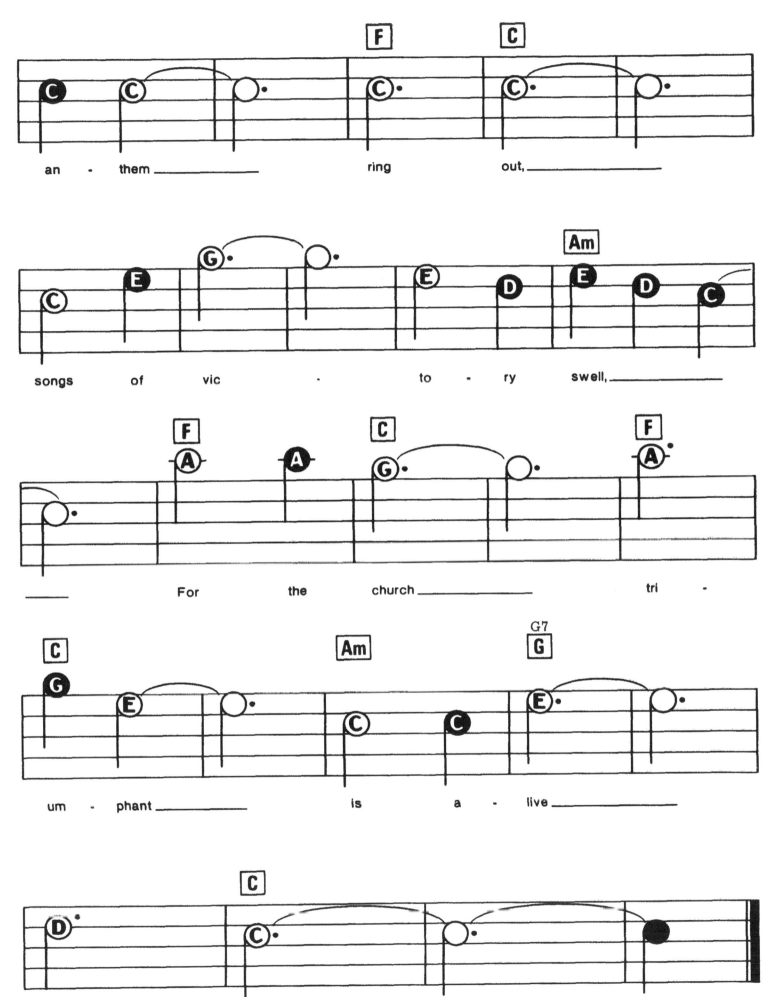

Come, Holy Spirit

Registration 3
Rhythm: Waltz

Words by William J. & Gloria Gaither
Music by William J. Gaither

19

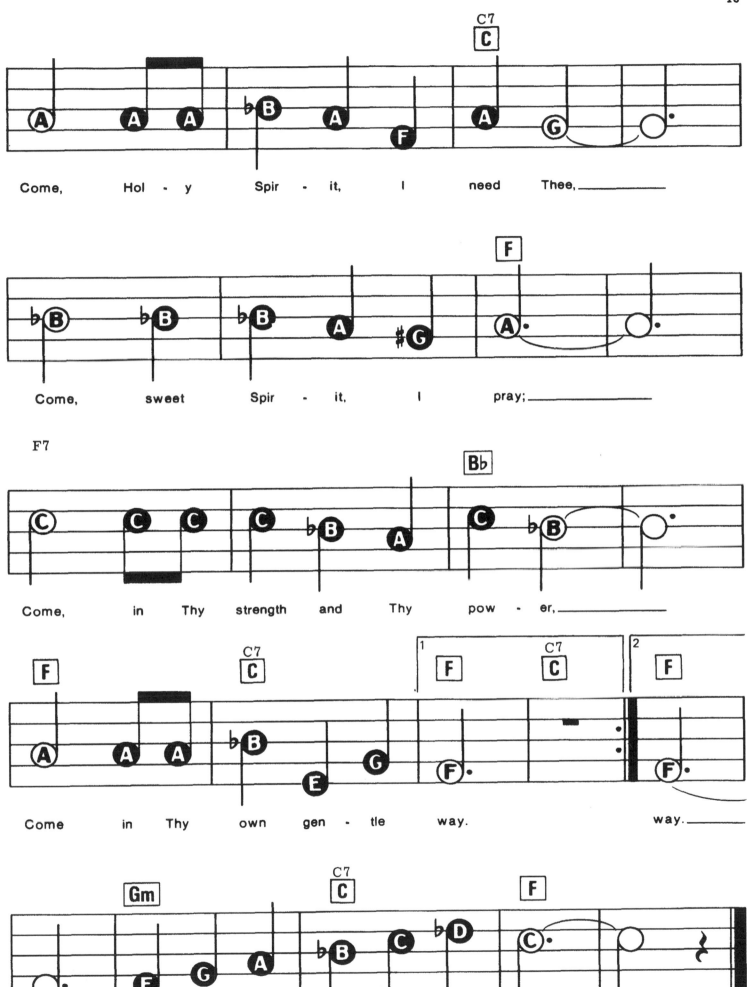

Dream On

Registration 8
Rhythm: Ballad or Slow Rock

Words by Gloria Gaither
Music by William J. Gaither and David Huntsinger

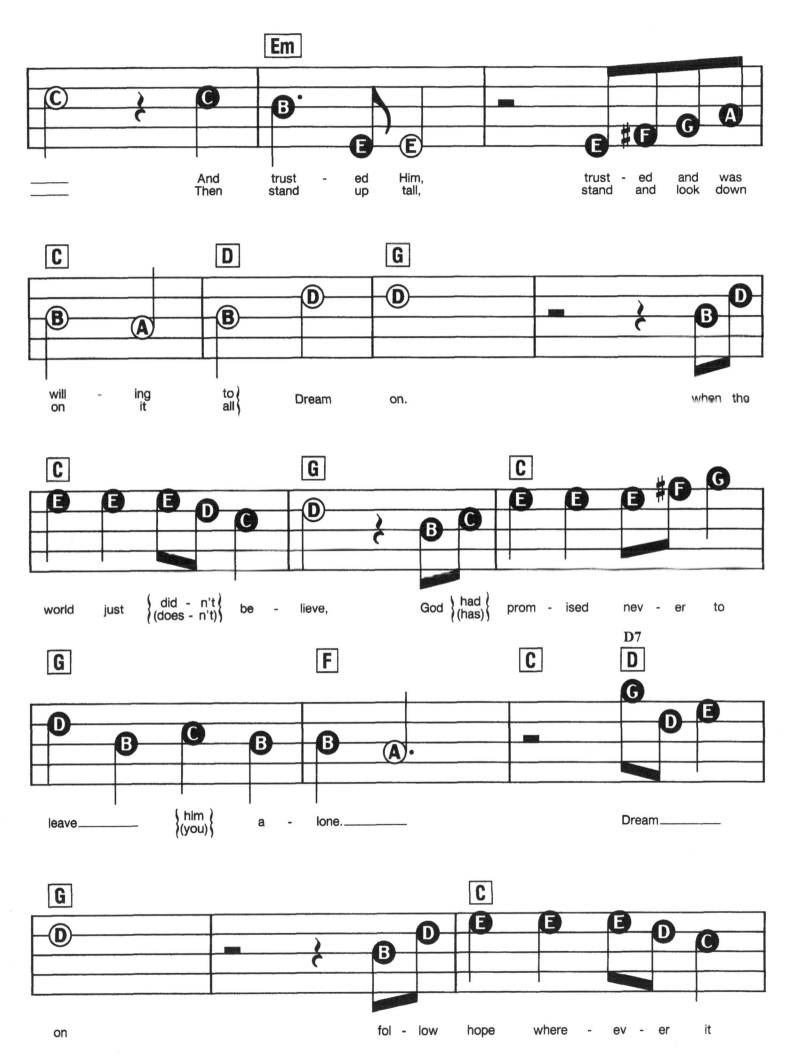

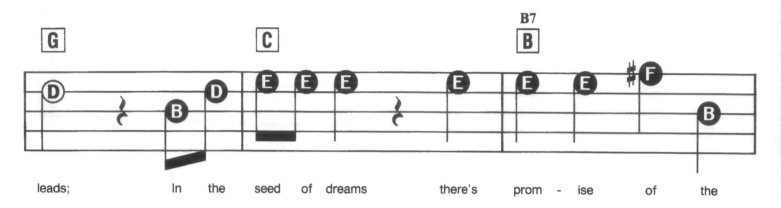

leads;   In   the   seed   of   dreams   there's   prom - ise   of   the

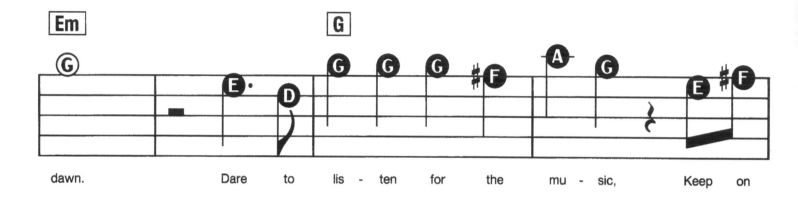

dawn.   Dare   to   lis - ten   for   the   mu - sic,   Keep   on

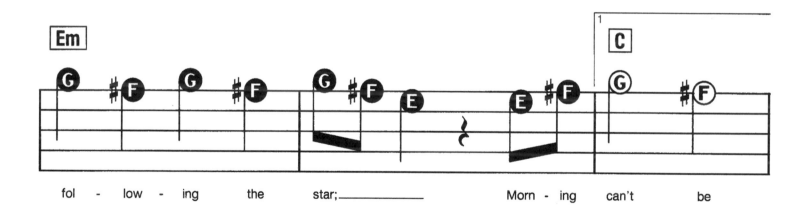

fol - low - ing   the   star;_____   Morn - ing   can't   be

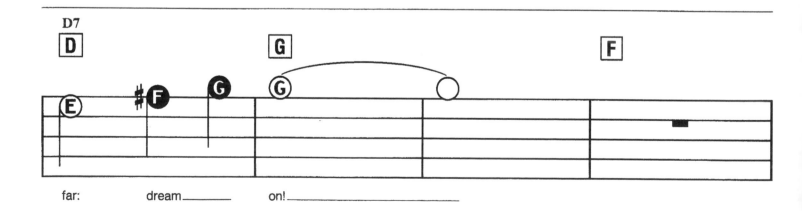

far: dream_____   on!_____

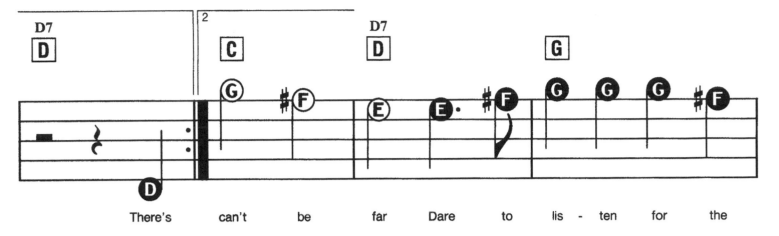

There's   can't   be   far   Dare   to   lis - ten   for   the

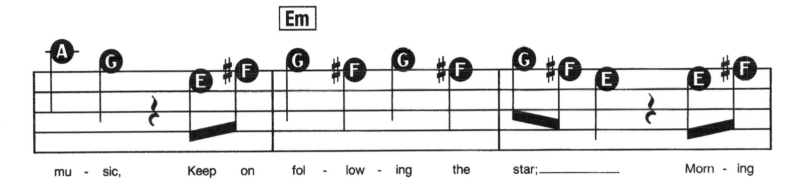

mu - sic,   Keep   on   fol - low - ing   the   star;＿＿＿   Morn - ing

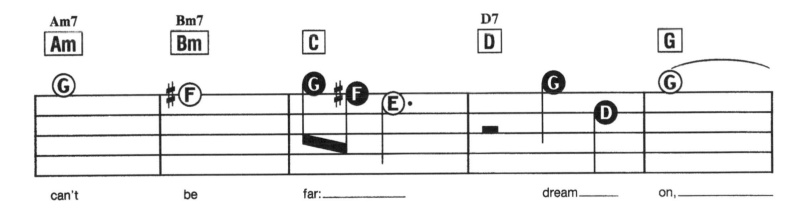

can't   be   far:＿＿＿   dream＿＿＿   on,＿＿＿

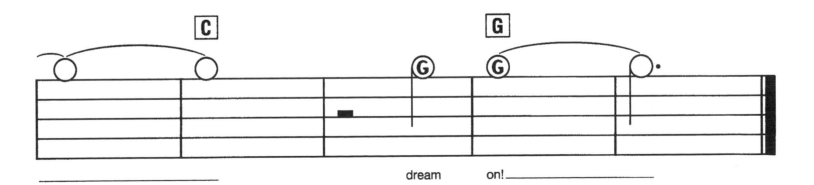

dream   on!＿＿＿

Even So, Lord Jesus, Come

Registration 3
Rhythm: Waltz

Words by William J. & Gloria Gaither
Music by William J. Gaither

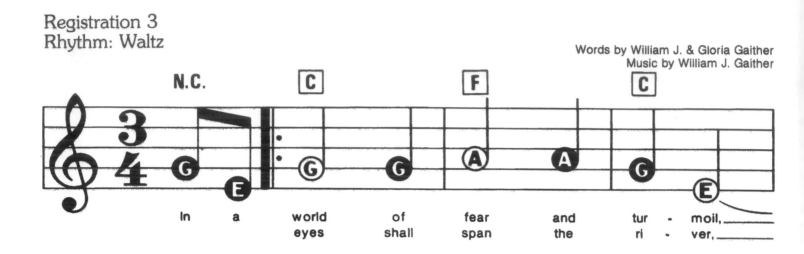

In a world of fear and tur - moil,_____
eyes shall span the ri - ver,_____

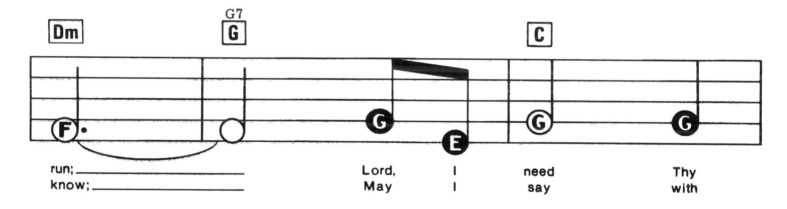

In a race that seems so hard to
When I gaze in - to the vast un -

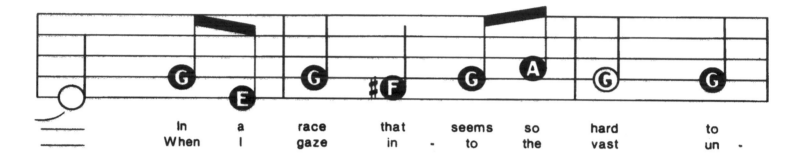

run;_____ Lord, I need Thy
know;_____ May I say with

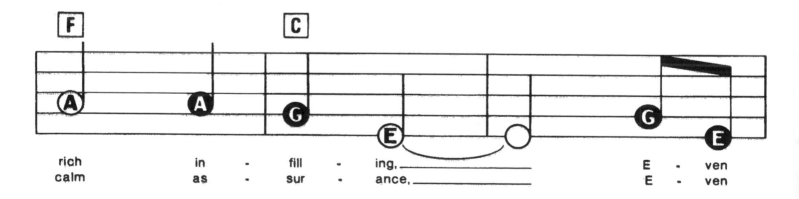

rich in - fill - ing,_____ E - ven
calm as - sur - ance,_____ E - ven

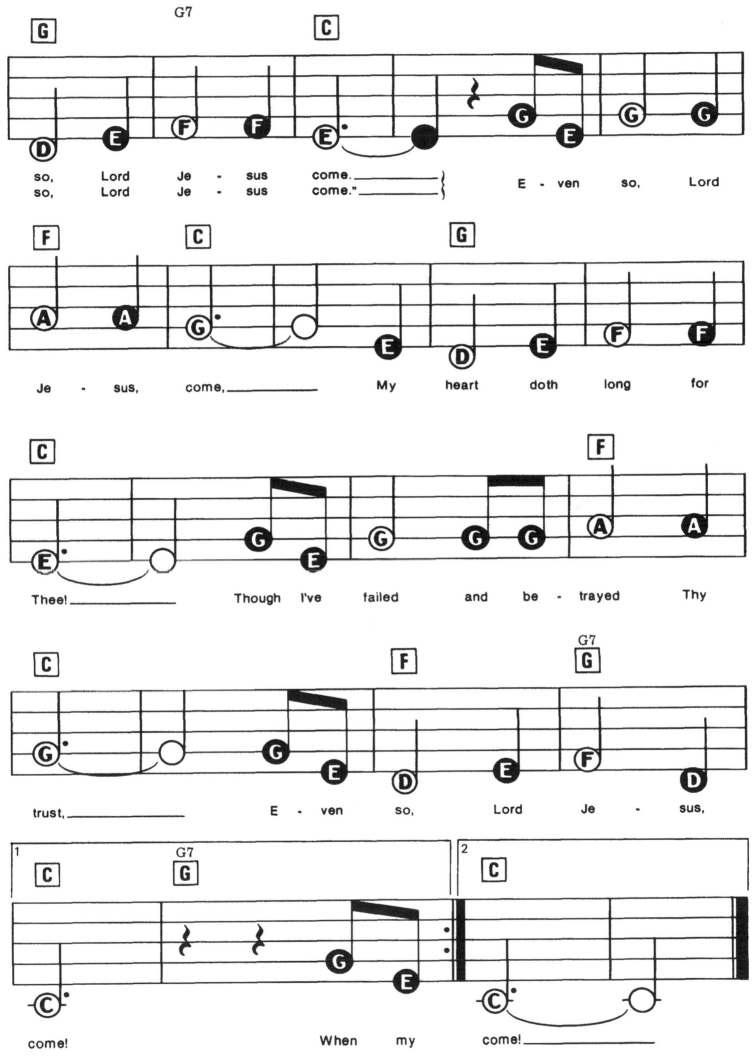

The Family Of God

Registration 2
Rhythm: Waltz

Words by William J. & Gloria Gaither
Music by William J. Gaither

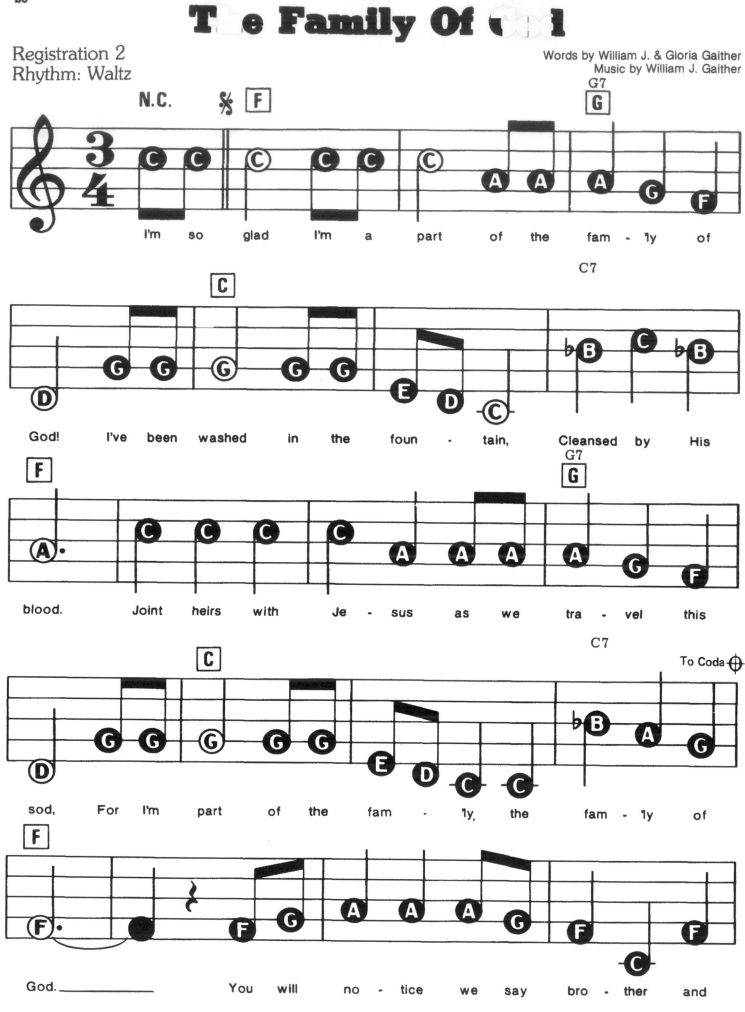

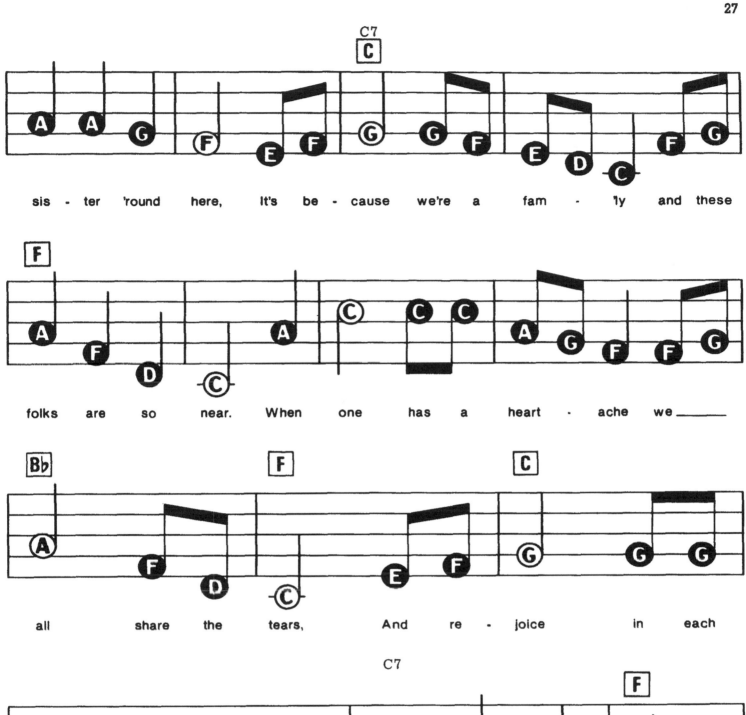

sis - ter 'round here, It's be - cause we're a fam - 'ly and these folks are so near. When one has a heart - ache we ____ all share the tears, And re - joice in each vic - t'ry in this fam - 'ly so dear. ____

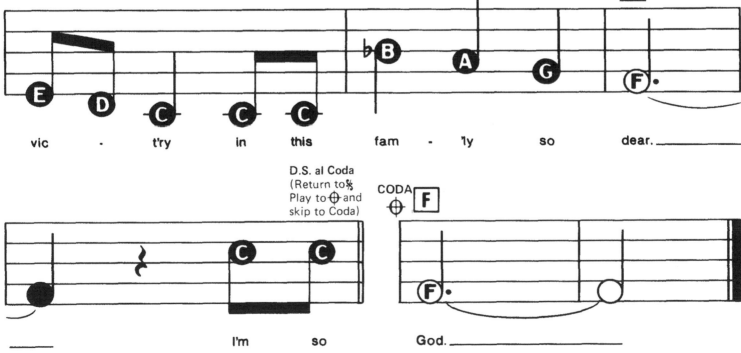

D.S. al Coda
(Return to %
Play to ⊕ and
skip to Coda)

CODA

____ I'm so God. ____

Fully Alive

Registration 5
Rhythm: Jazz Rock or Rock

Words by Gloria Gaither
Music by William J. Gaither

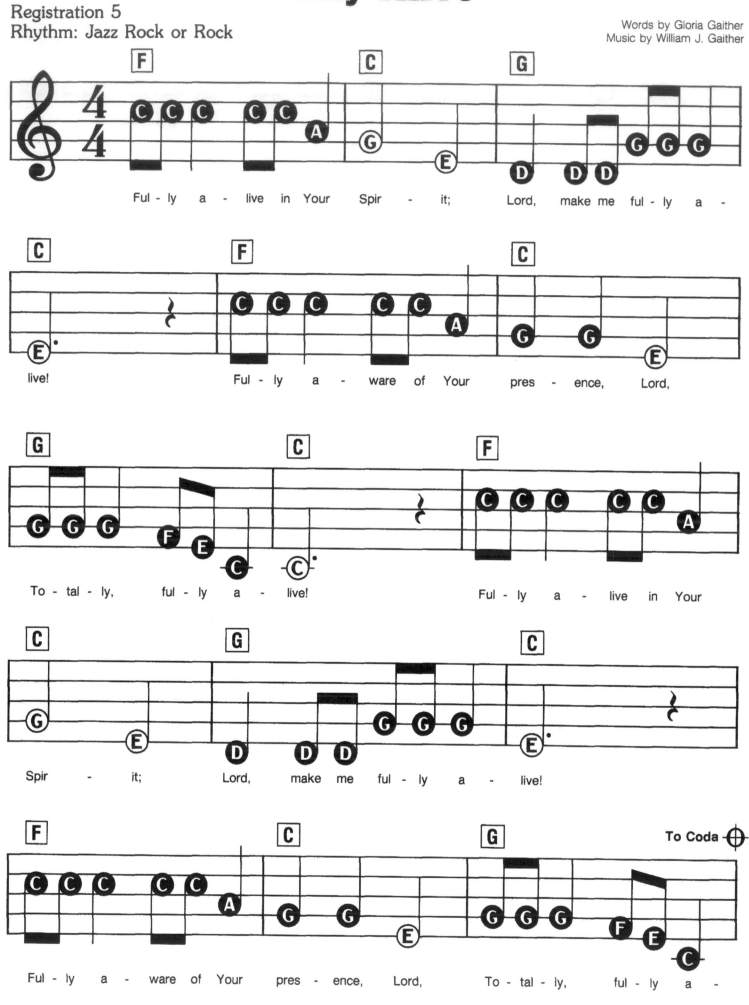

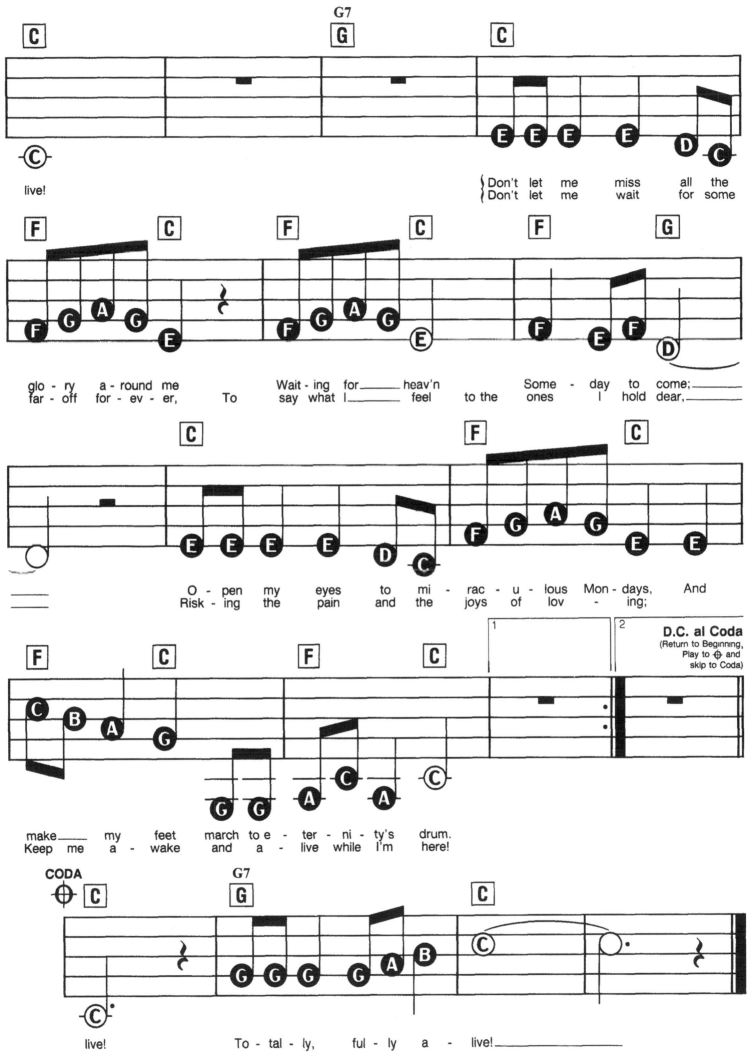

Feeling At Home
In The Presence Of Jesus

Registration 4
Rhythm: Fox Trot or Swing

Words and Music by
William J. Gaither

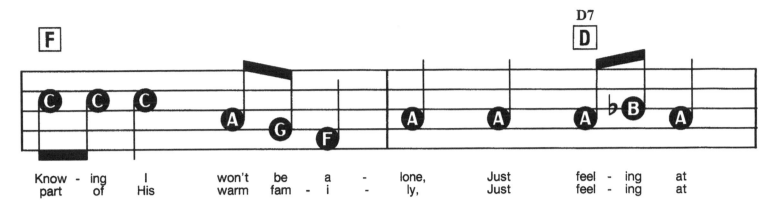

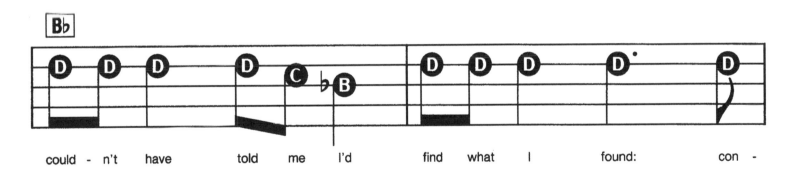

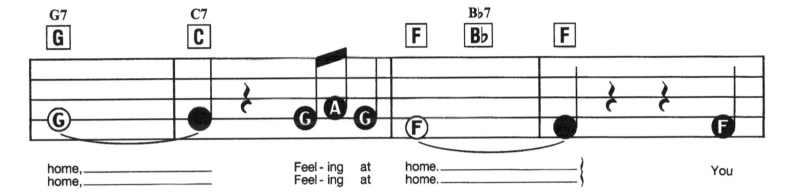

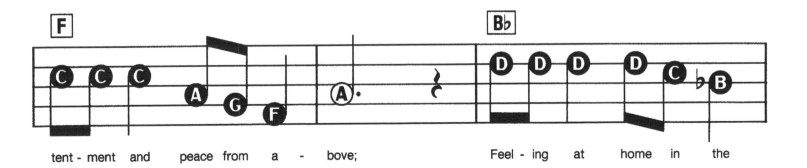

I Am A Promise

Registration 4
Rhythm: Rock or Jazz Rock

Words by William J. and Gloria Gaither
Music by William J. Gaither

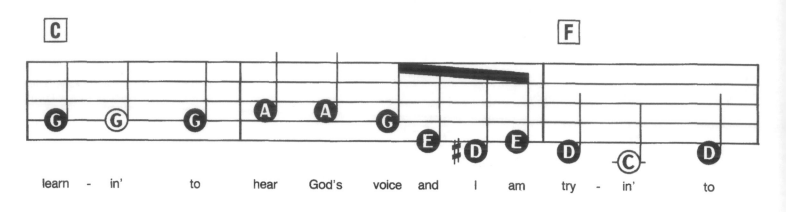

learn - in'   to   hear   God's   voice   and   I   am   try - in'   to

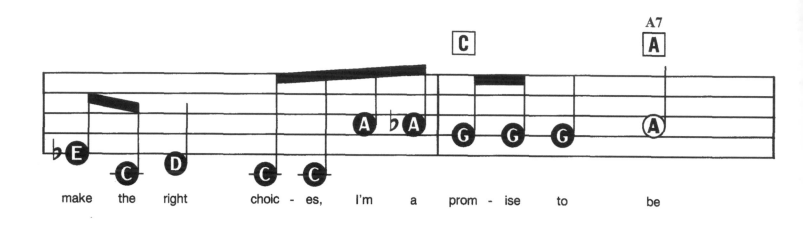

make   the   right   choic - es,   I'm   a   prom - ise   to   be

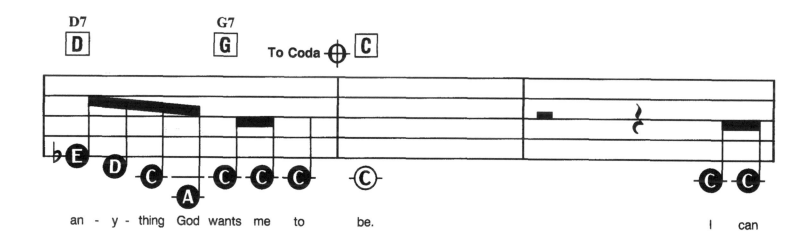

an - y - thing   God   wants   me   to   be.   I   can

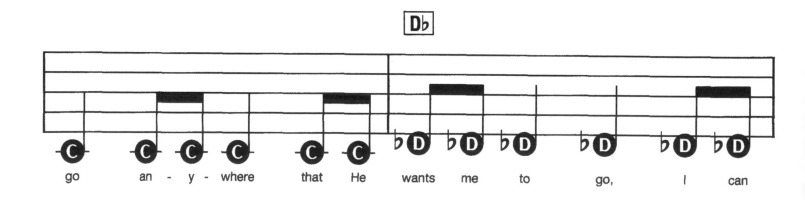

go   an - y - where   that   He   wants   me   to   go,   I   can

Gentle Shepherd

Registration 6
Rhythm: Ballad or Slow Rock

Words by William J. and Gloria Gaither
Music by William J. Gaither

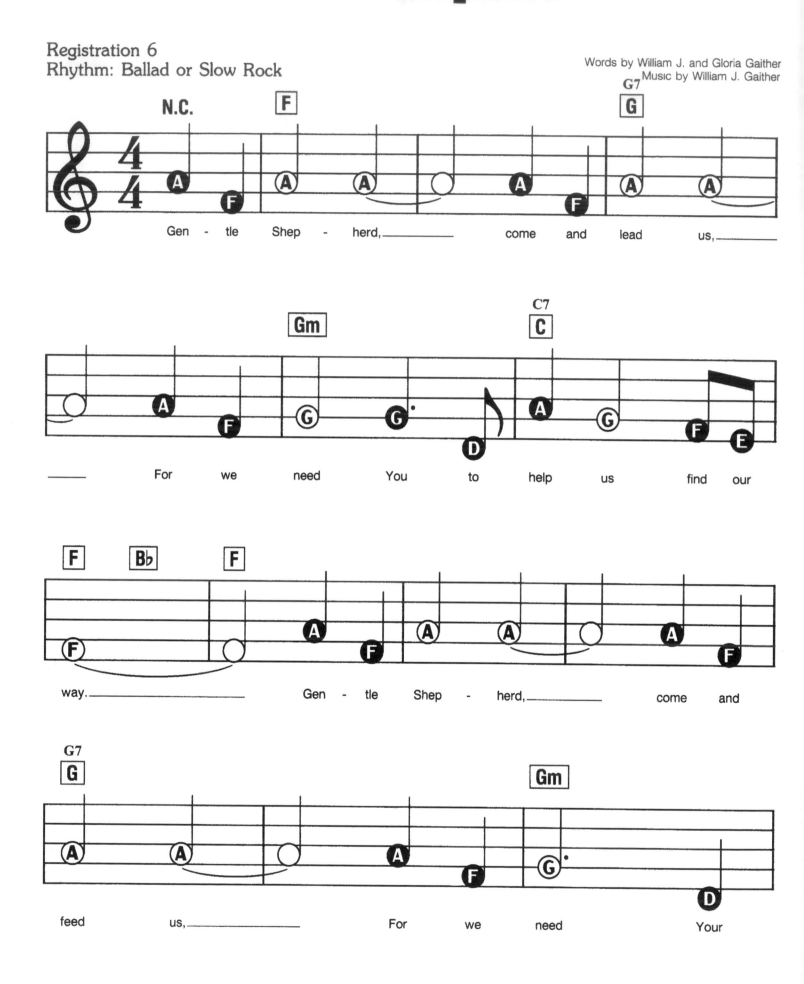

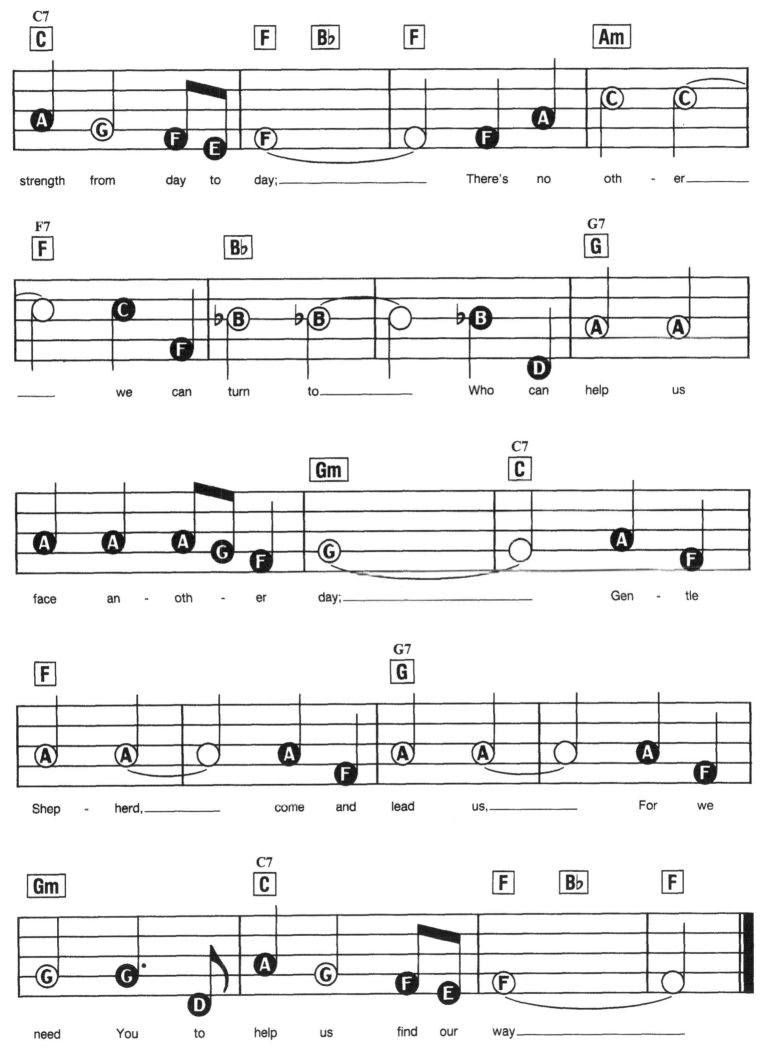

Get All Excited

Registration 4
Rhythm: Rock

Words and Music by
William J. Gaither

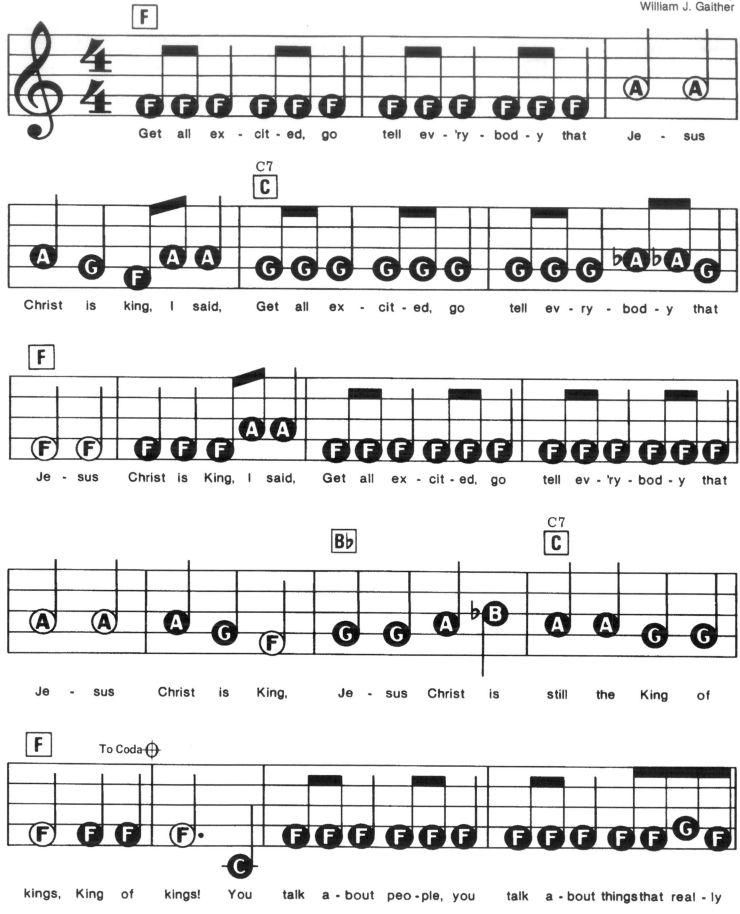

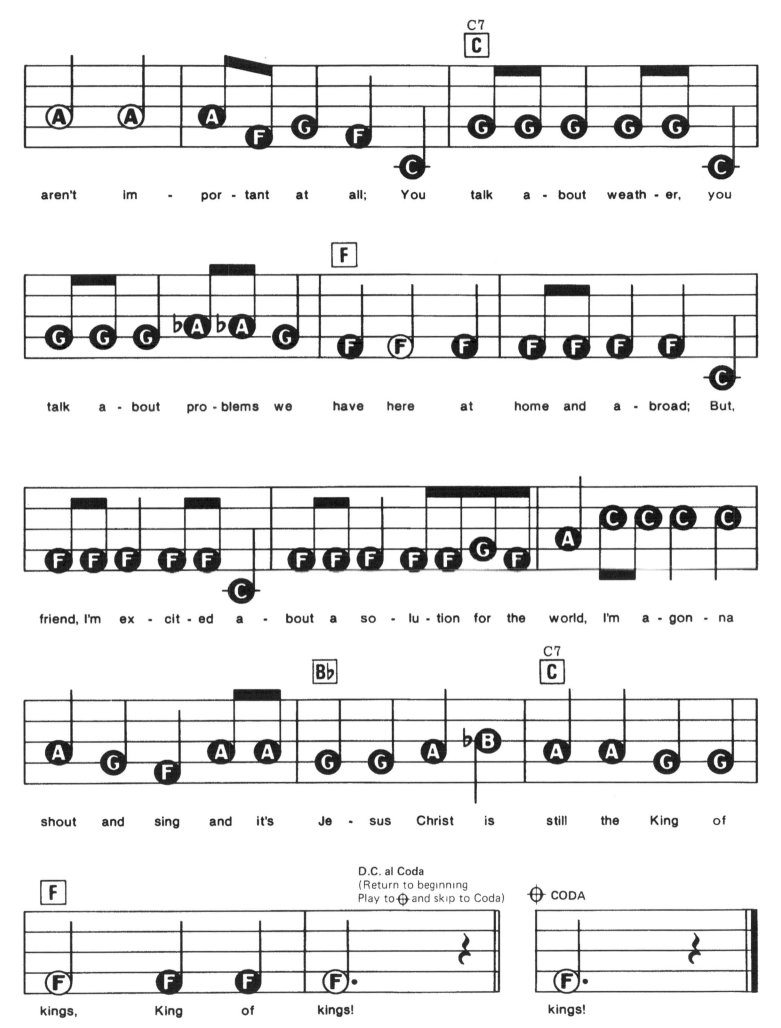

He Touched Me

Registration 2
Rhythm: Waltz

Words and Music by
William J. Gaither

Shack - led by a heav - y bur - den ____
Since I met this bless - ed Sav - ior ____

____ 'Neath a load of guilt and shame ____
Since He cleansed and made me whole ____

____ Then the hand of Je - sus touched me ____
____ I will nev - er cease to praise Him ____

____ and now I am no long - er the same ____
____ I'll shout it while e - ter - ni - ty rolls ____

41

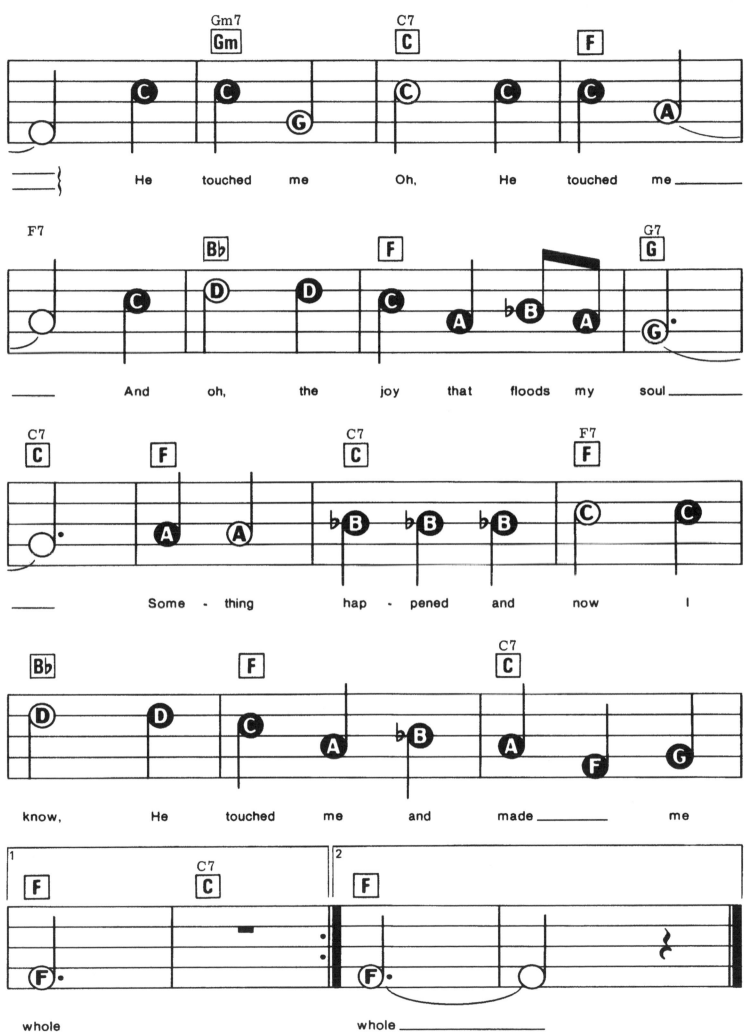

He's Still The King Of Kings
(And Lord Of Lords)

Registration 2
Rhythm: Waltz

Words by William J. & Gloria Gaither
Music by William J. Gaither

43

I Believe In A Hill Called Mt. Calvary

Registration 2
Rhythm: Waltz

Words by W. Dale Oldham, William J. & Gloria Gaither
Music by William J. Gaither

45

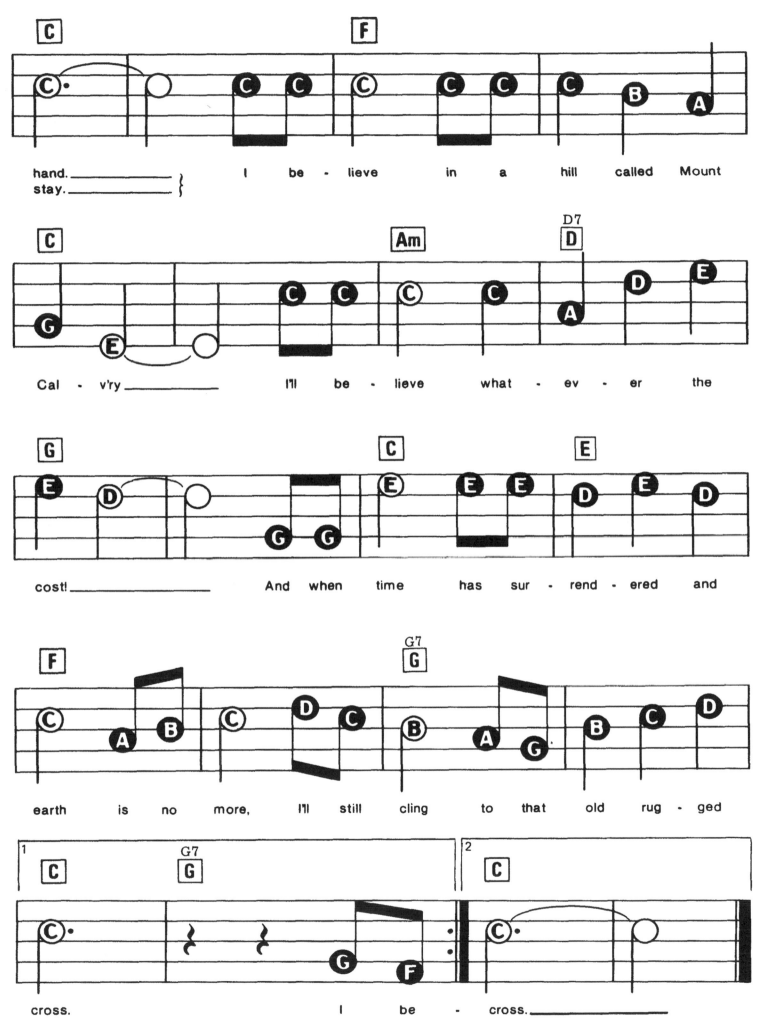

I Came To Praise The Lord

Registration 4
Rhythm: Rock

Words and Music by
William J. Gaither

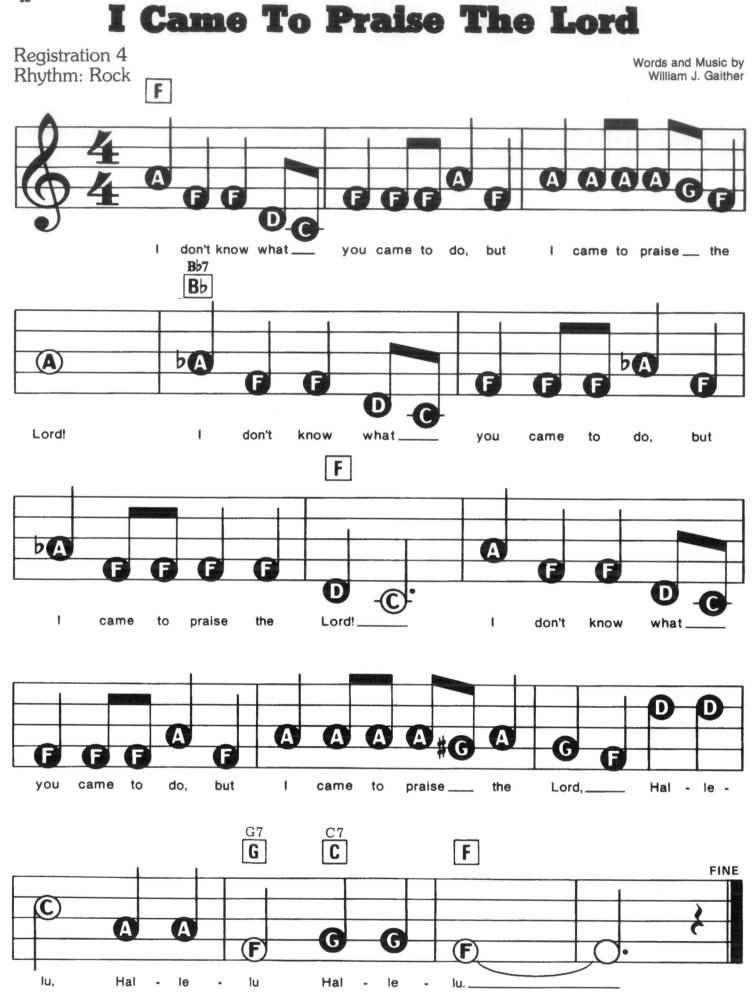

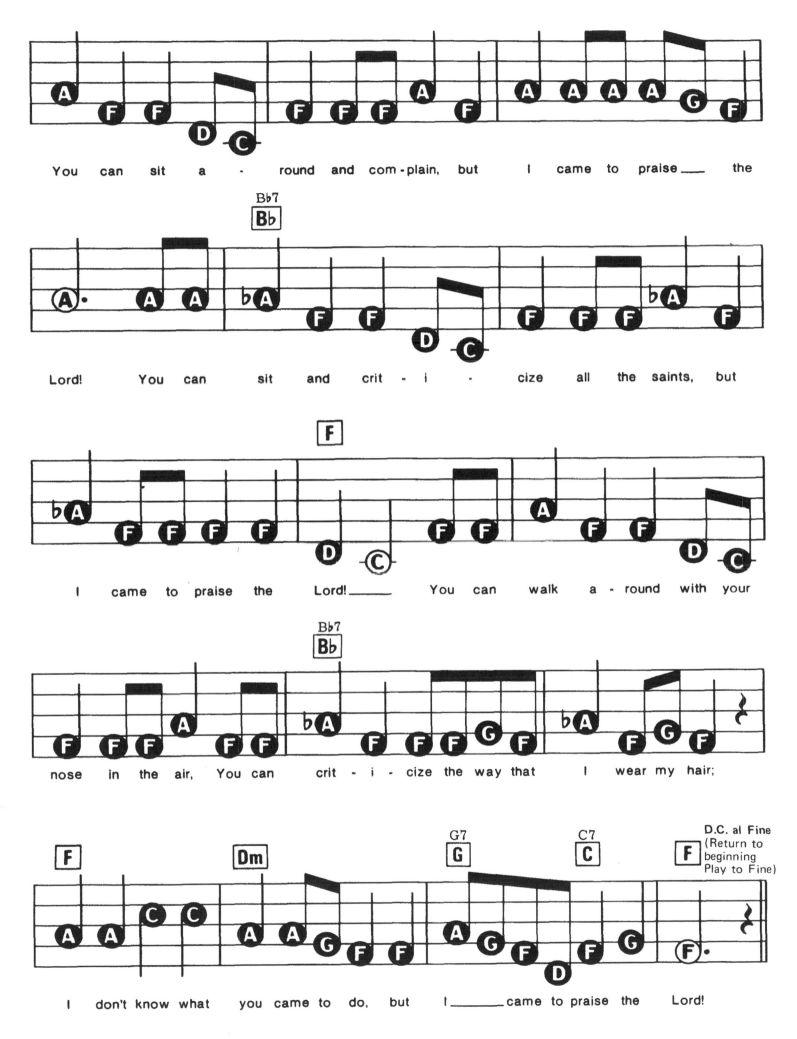

I Could Never Outlove The Lord

Registration 6
Rhythm: Waltz

Words by William J. & Gloria Gaither
Music by William J. Gaither

N.C. F

There've been / showed us   times   when / that   giv / on - ing / ly   and / thro'

Bb   F   C

lov - ing / dy - ing   brought / we   pain, / live,   And I / And He   prom - ised / gave _____   I would / when it

C7   F

nev - er / seemed there   let / was _____   it   hap - pen / noth - ing   a - / to   gain; / give;   But I / He _____   found / loved _____   out   that / when

F7   Bb   Gm7 Gm   C

lov - ing / lov - ing   was / brought   well worth / heart - ache   the / and   risk, / loss;   And that / He for - gave   e - ven / from   in / an

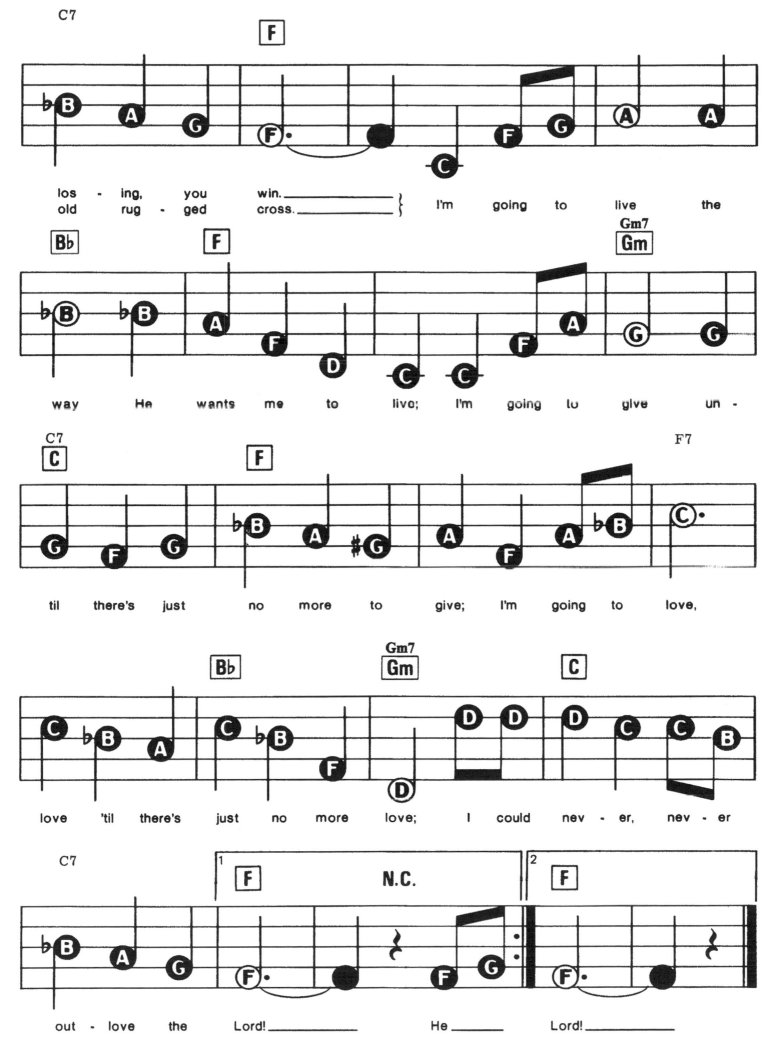

I Walked Today Where Jesus Walks

Registration: 3
Rhythm: Ballad or Slow Rock

Words by Gloria Gaither
Music by Greg Nelson

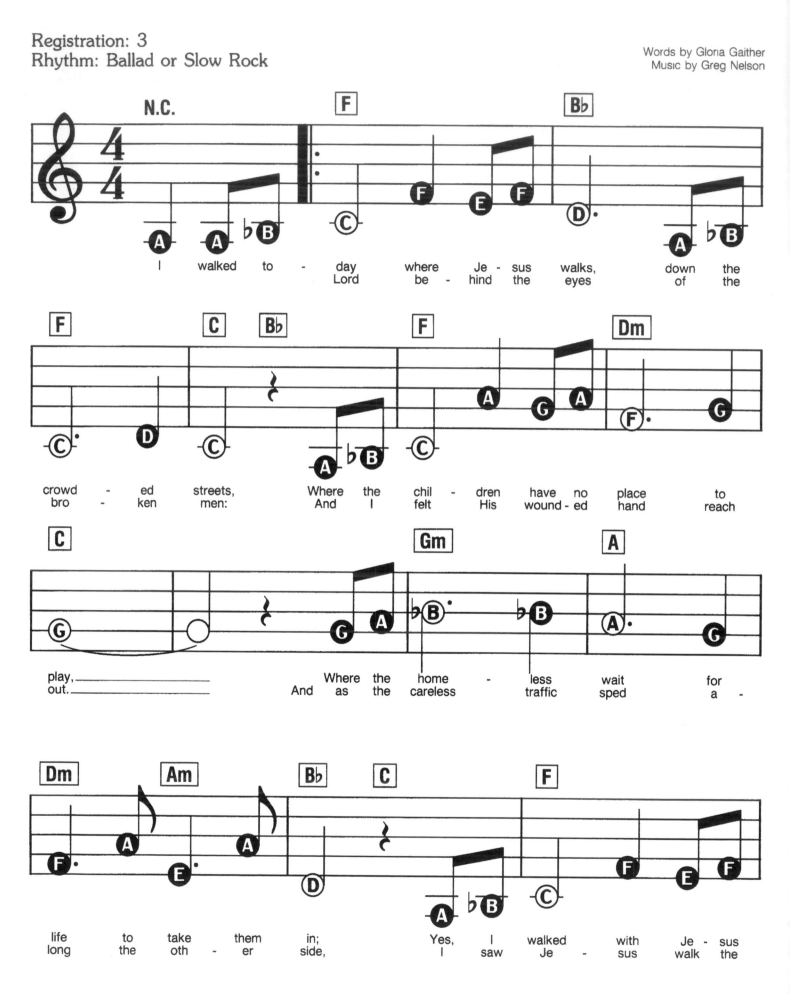

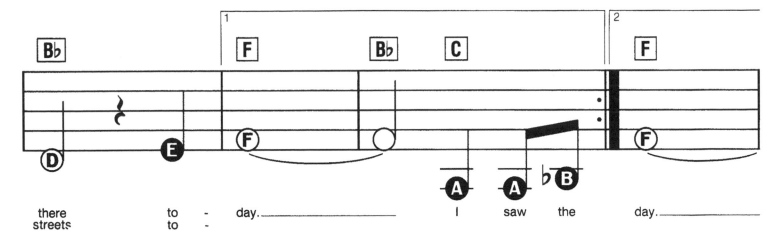

there streets to - day. I saw the day.

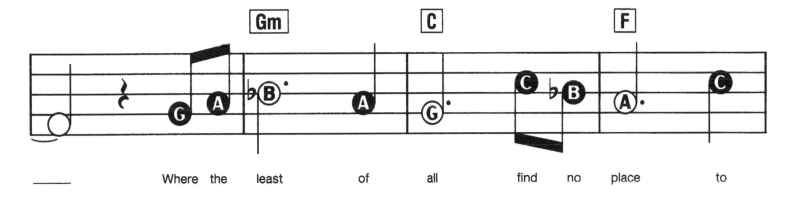

Where the least of all find no place to

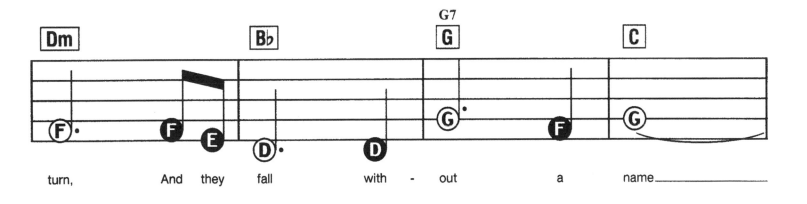

turn, And they fall with - out a name

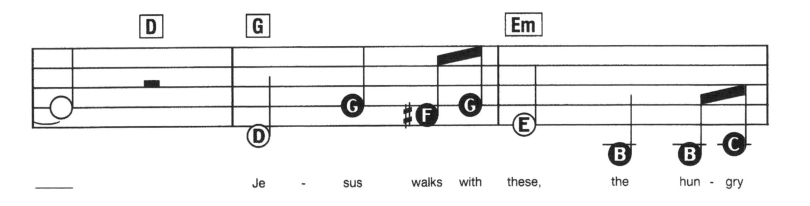

Je - sus walks with these, the hun - gry

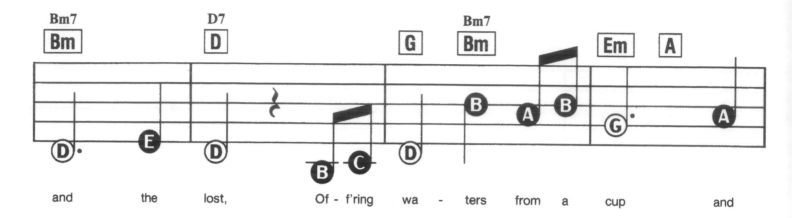

and the lost, Of-f'ring wa - ters from a cup and

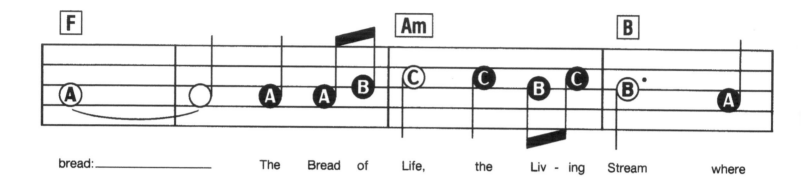

bread:_____ The Bread of Life, the Liv - ing Stream where

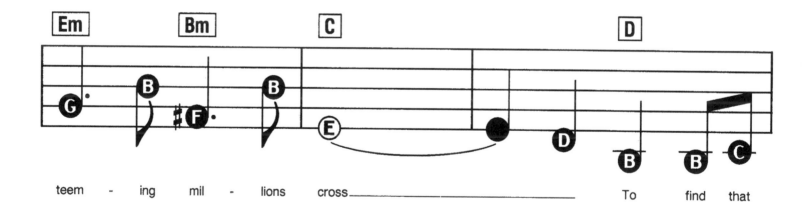

teem - ing mil - lions cross_____ To find that

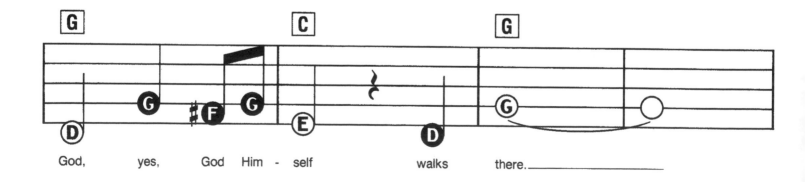

God, yes, God Him - self walks there._____

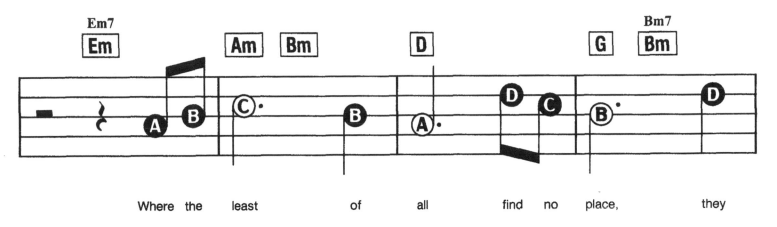

Where the least of all find no place, they

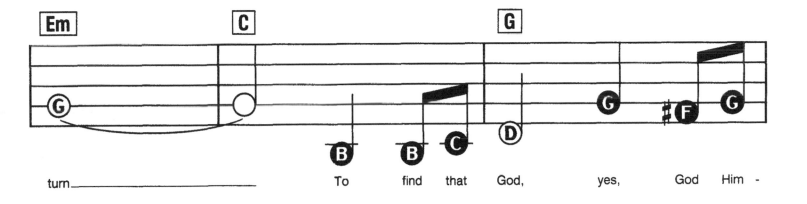

turn_____ To find that God, yes, God Him -

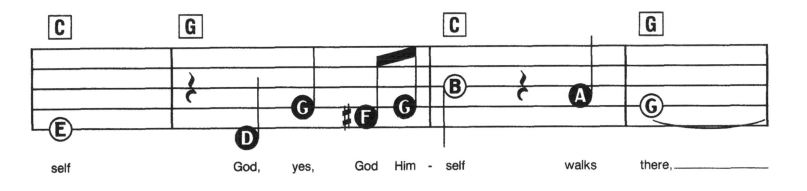

self God, yes, God Him - self walks there,_____

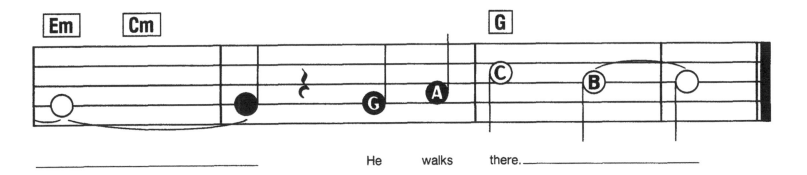

_____ He walks there._____

I Will Serve Thee

Registration 3
Rhythm: Rock

Words by William J. & Gloria Gaither
Music by William J. Gaither

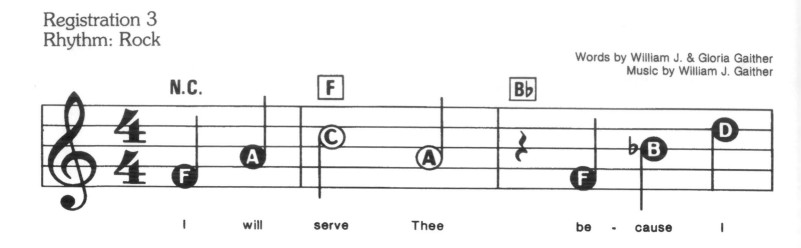

I will serve Thee be - cause I

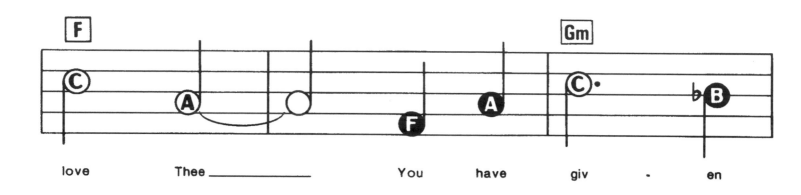

love Thee _____ You have giv - en

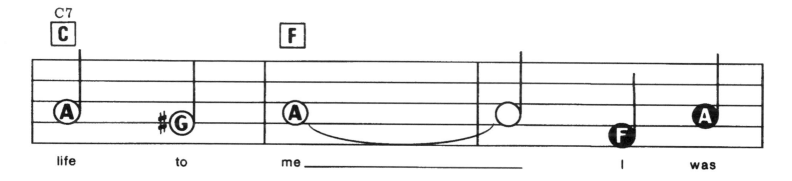

life to me _____ I was

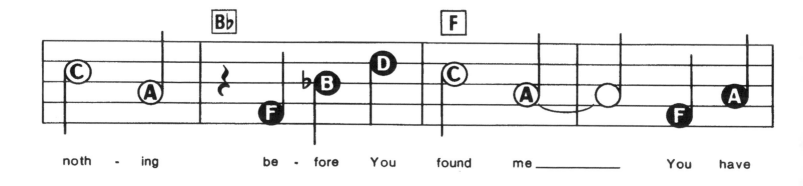

noth - ing be - fore You found me _____ You have

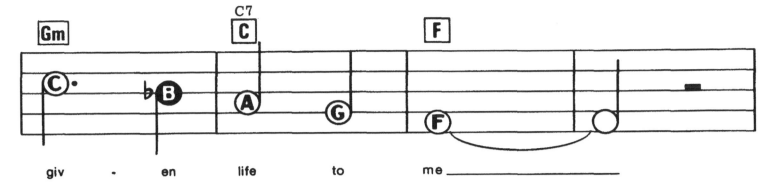

giv - en life to me _____

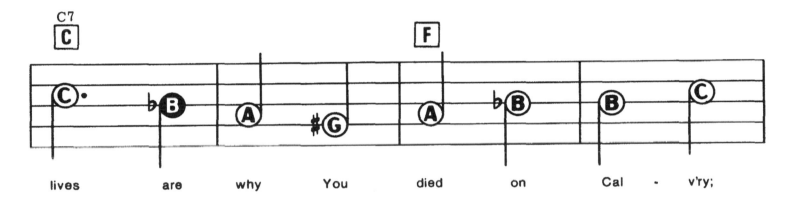

Heart - aches _____ bro - ken piec - es _____ Ru - ined

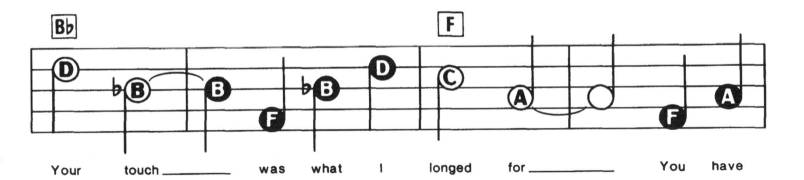

lives are why You died on Cal - v'ry;

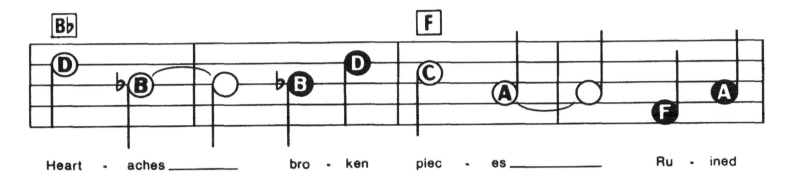

Your touch _____ was what I longed for _____ You have

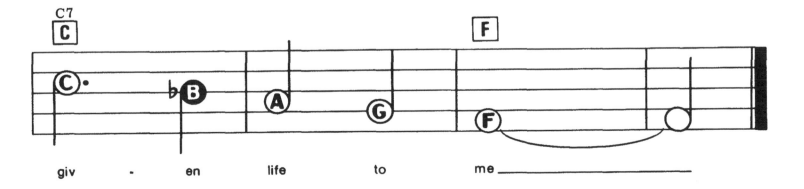

giv - en life to me _____

I've Been To Calvary

Registration 6
Rhythm: Waltz

Words and Music by
William J. Gaither

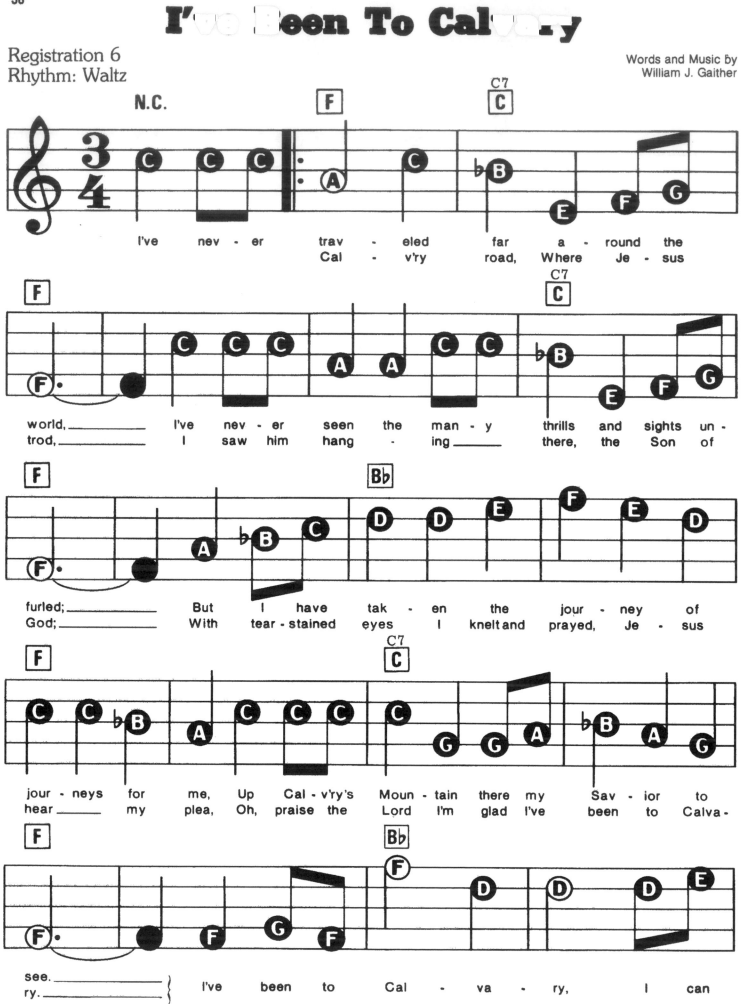

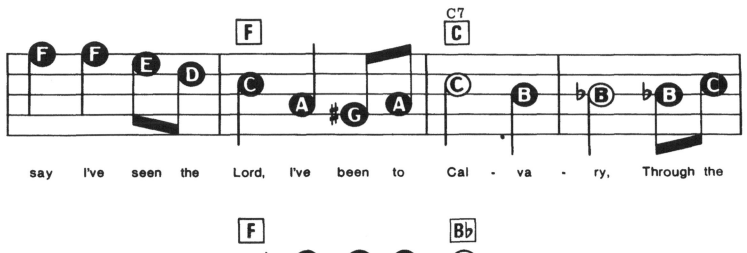

say I've seen the Lord, I've been to Cal - va - ry, Through the

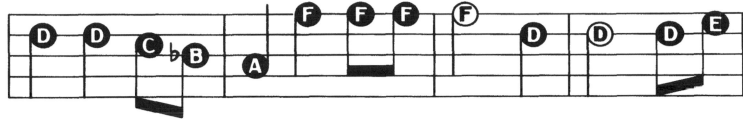

wit - ness of His word, Each day at Cal - va - ry, What a

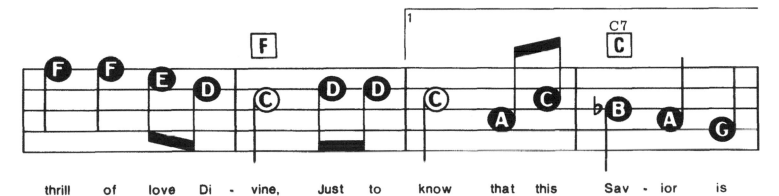

thrill of love Di - vine, Just to know that this Sav - ior is

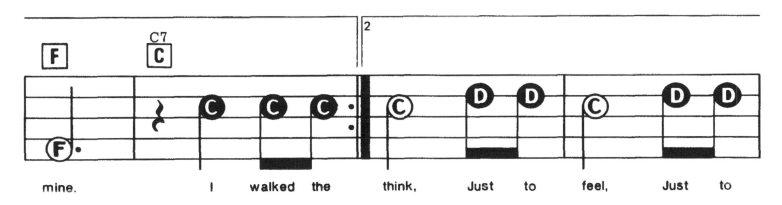

mine. I walked the think, Just to feel, Just to

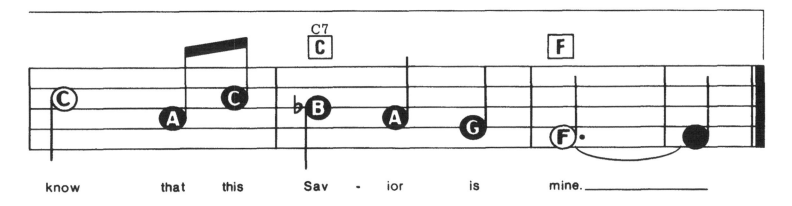

know that this Sav - ior is mine.

I've Just Seen Jesus

Registration: 3
Rhythm: Ballad or Slow Rock

Words by Gloria Gaither
Music by William J. Gaither and Danny Daniels

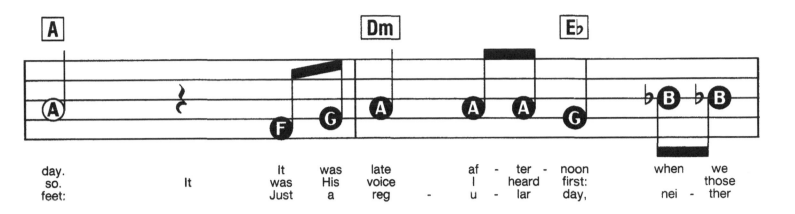

day. It was late af - ter - noon when we
so. It was His voice I heard first: those
feet: Just a reg - u - lar day, nei - ther

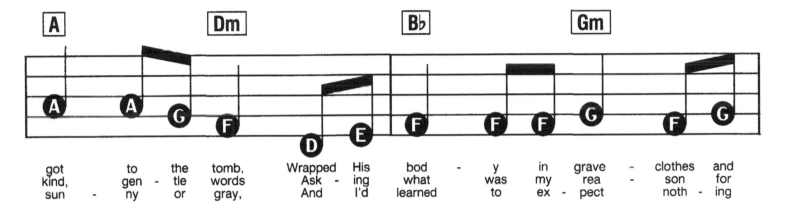

got to the tomb, Wrapped His bod - y in grave - clothes and
kind, gen - tle words Ask - ing what was my rea - son for
sun - ny or gray, And I'd learned to ex - pect noth - ing

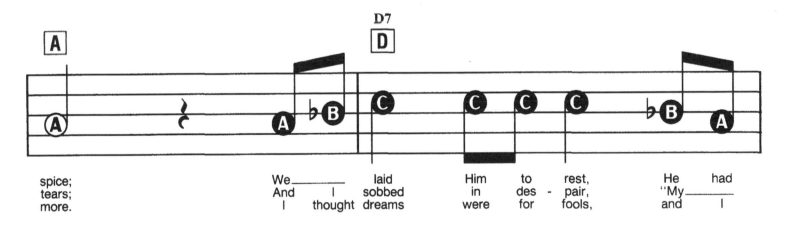

spice; We___ laid Him to rest, He had
tears; And I sobbed in des - pair, "My___
more. I thought dreams were for fools, and I

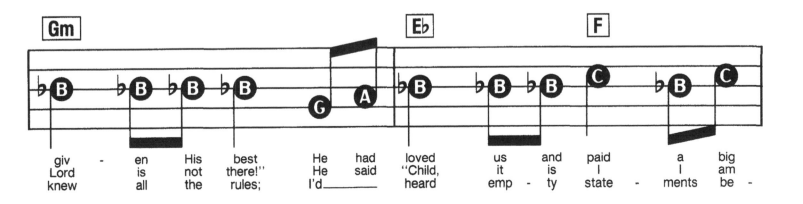

giv - en His best He had loved us and paid a big
Lord is not there!" He had said "Child, it is I___ am
knew all the rules; I'd___ heard emp - ty state - ments be -

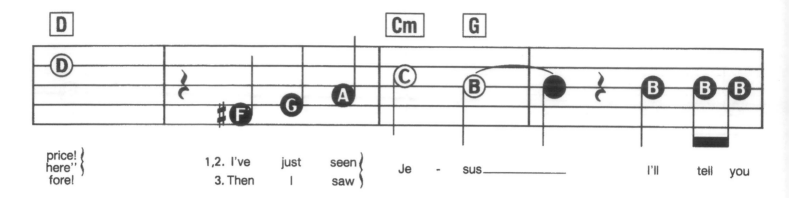

price! }
here" } 1,2. I've just seen } Je - sus___ I'll tell you
fore! } 3. Then I saw }

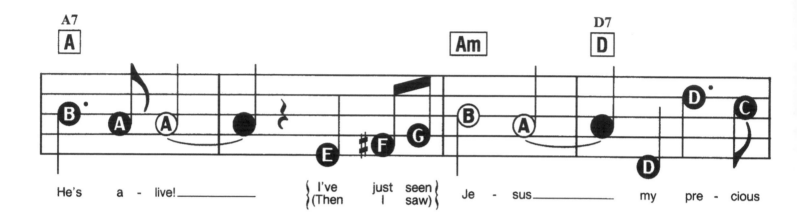

He's a - live!___ } I've just seen } Je - sus___ my pre - cious
(Then I saw) }

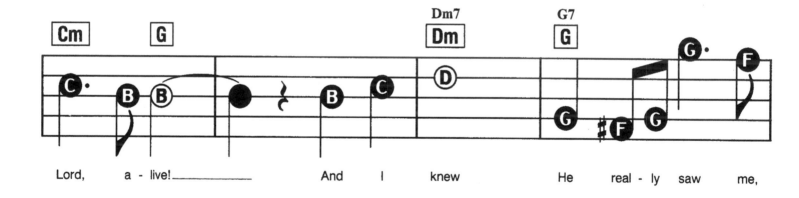

Lord, a - live!___ And I knew He real - ly saw me,

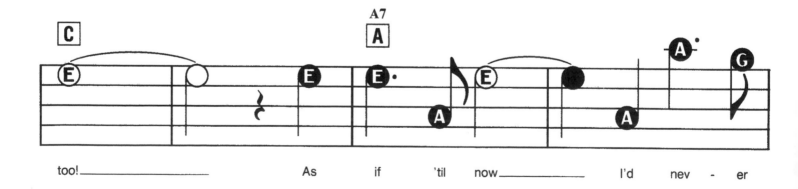

too!___ As if 'til now___ I'd nev - er

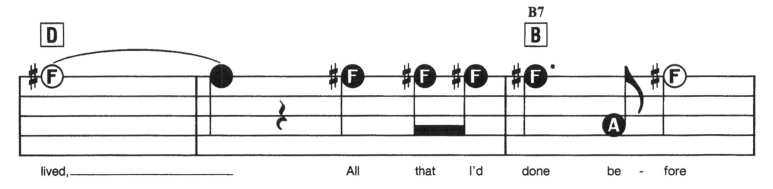

lived,_____ All that I'd done be - fore

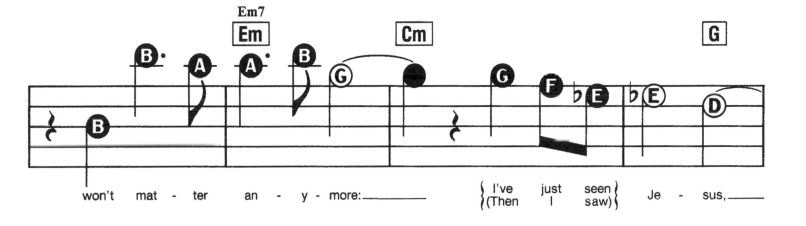

won't mat - ter an - y-more:_____ { I've just seen / (Then I saw) } Je - sus,____

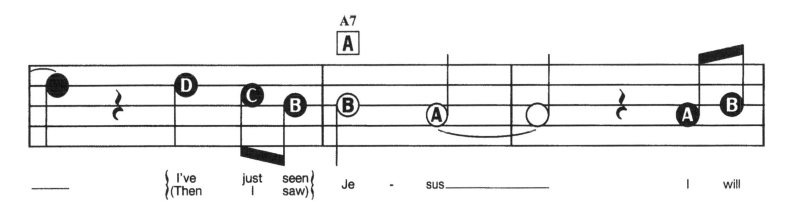

____ { I've just seen / (Then I saw) } Je - sus_____ I will

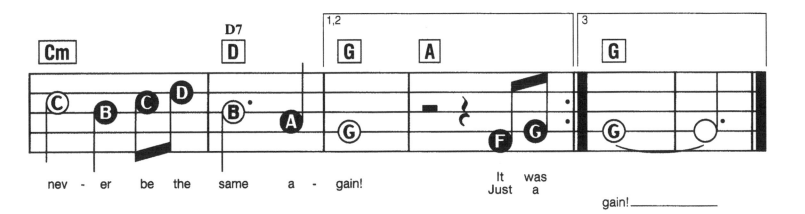

nev - er be the same a - gain! It was / Just a

gain!_____

If It Keeps Gettin' Better

Registration 3
Rhythm: Swing

Words and Music by
William J. Gaither

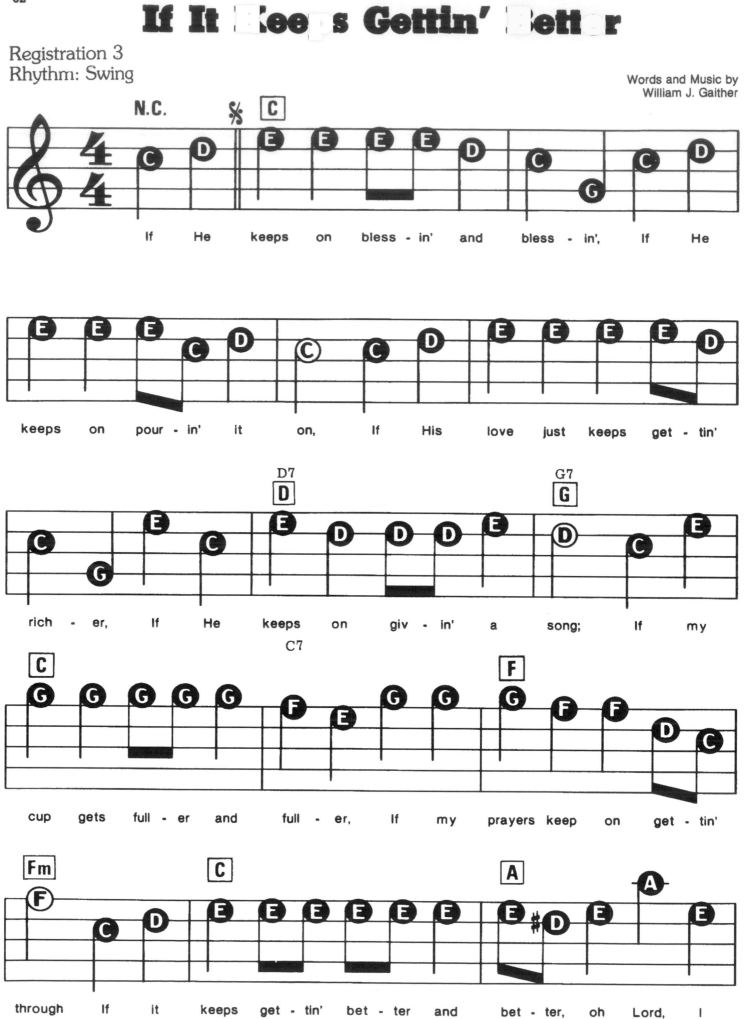

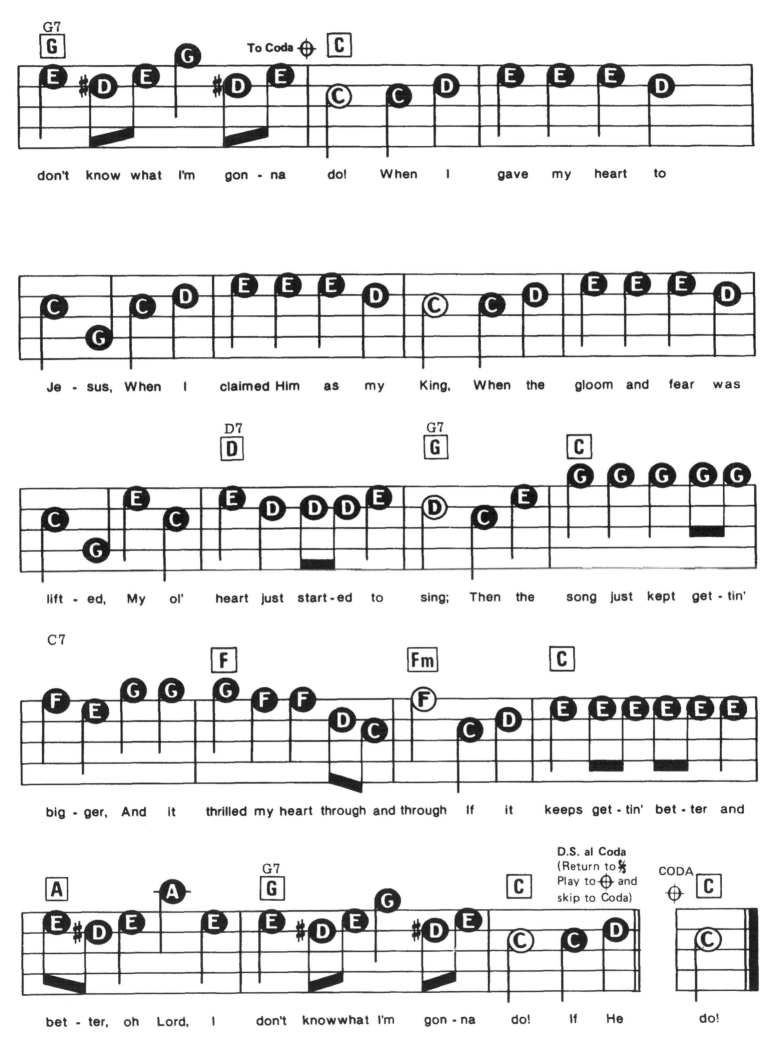

In The Upper Room

Registration 2
Rhythm: Waltz

Words and Music by
William J. Gaither

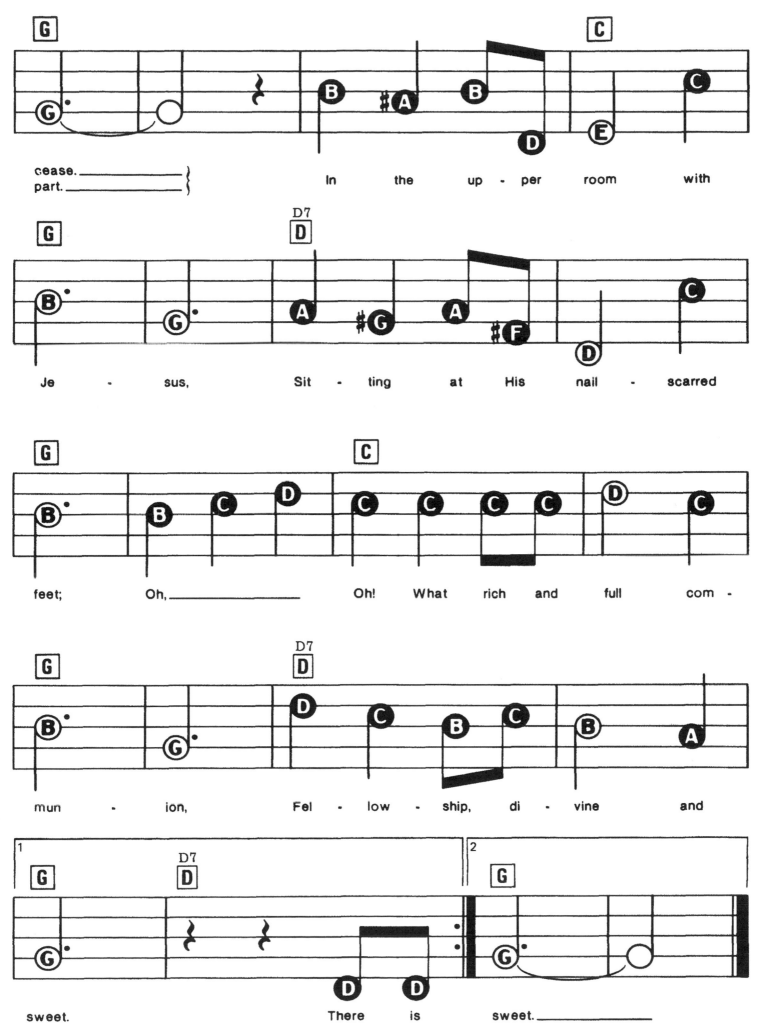

I Will Praise Him

Registration 5
Rhythm: 8 Beat or Rock

Words by Gloria Gaither and John W. Thompson
Music by John W. Thompson

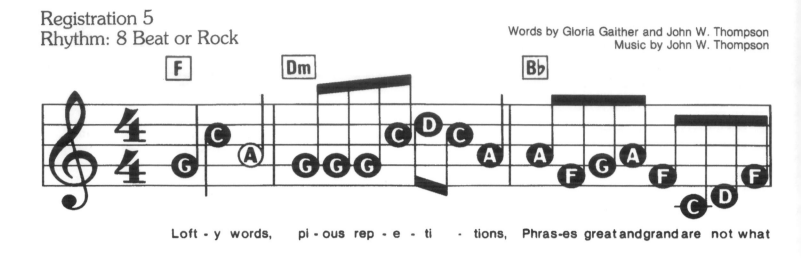

Loft - y words, pi - ous rep - e - ti - tions, Phras - es great and grand are not what

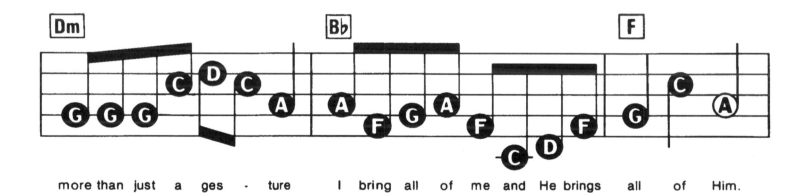

He de - mands; O - pen hands are

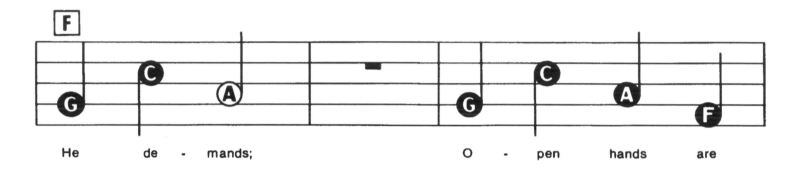

more than just a ges - ture I bring all of me and He brings all of Him.

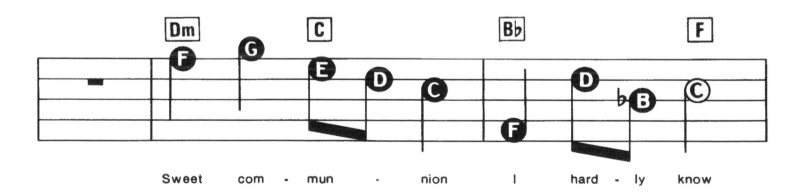

Sweet com - mun - nion I hard - ly know

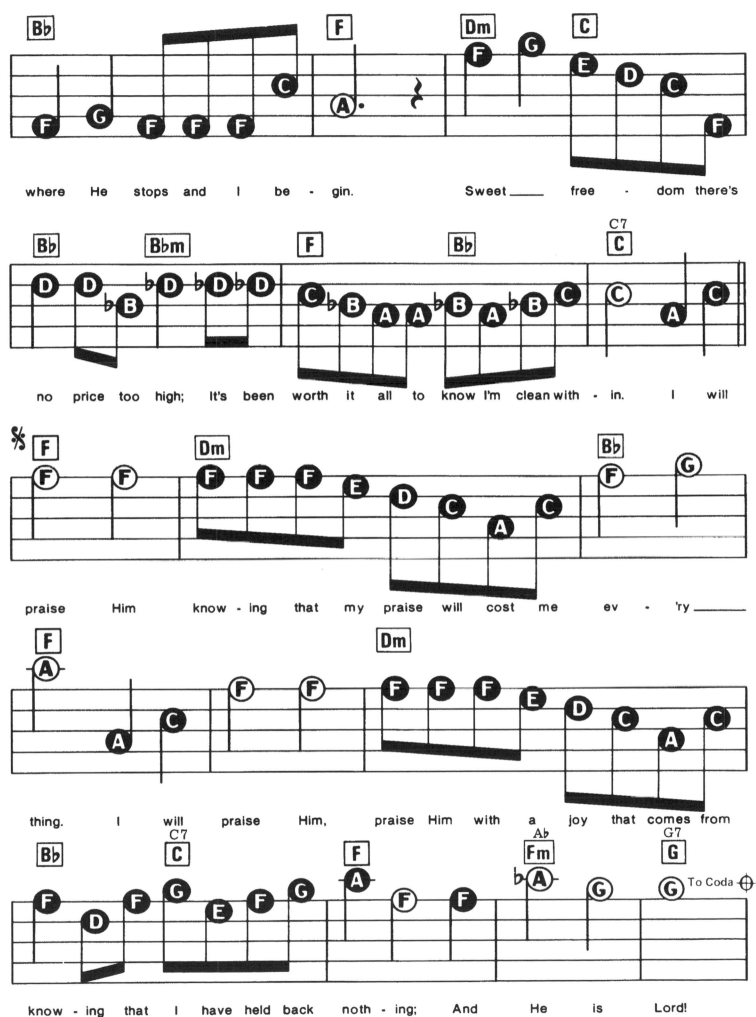

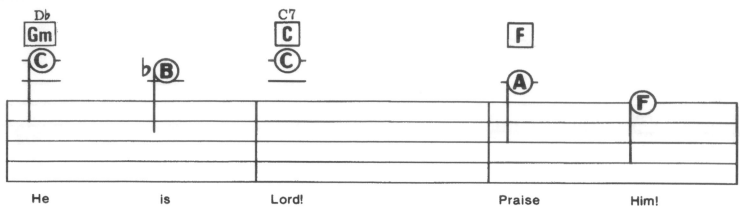

He   is   Lord!   Praise   Him!

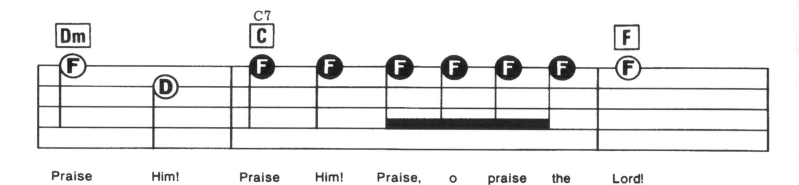

Praise   Him!   Praise   Him!   Praise,   o   praise   the   Lord!

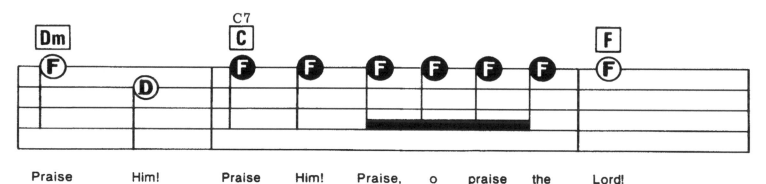

Praise   Him!   Praise   Him!   Praise,   o   praise   the   Lord!

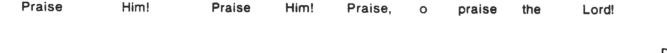

D.S. al Coda
(Return to 𝄋
Play to ⊕ and
skip to Coda)

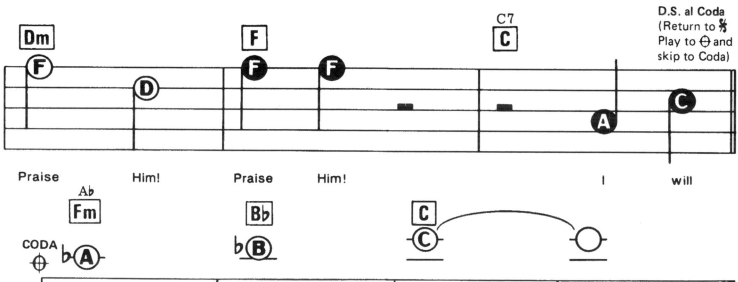

Praise   Him!   Praise   Him!   I   will

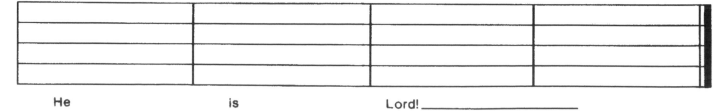

He   is   Lord! _____

It Is Finished

Registration 3
Rhythm: Waltz

Words by William J. & Gloria Gaither
Music by William J. Gaither

gain of man's soul or his loss._____ The

earth shakes with the force of the con - flict,_____ And the
heard shakes that with the _____ King of the A - ges,_____ Had _____

sun re - fu - ses to shine;_____ For
fought all the bat - tles for me;_____ And

there hangs God's Son in the bal - ance,_____ And
vic - t'ry was mine for the claim - ing,_____ And

then through the dark - ness He cries:_____ } "It is
now, praise His name, I am free._____ }

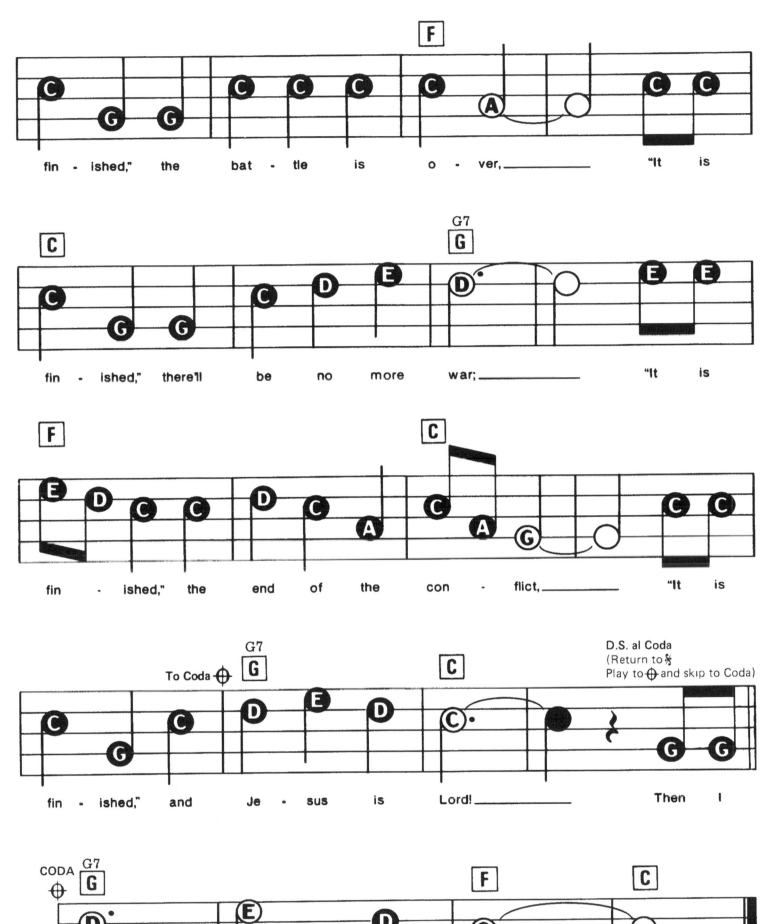

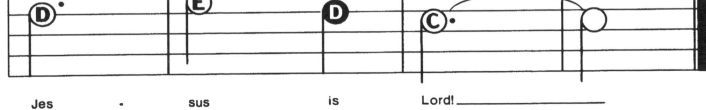

It Will Be Worth It All

Registration 6
Rhythm: Waltz

Words and Music by
William J. Gaither

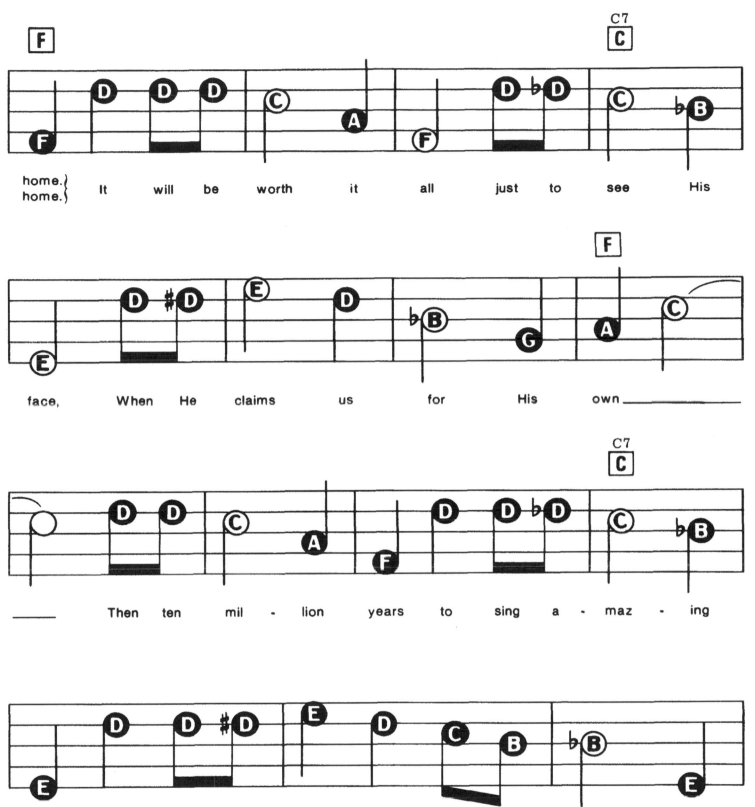

home.}
home.} It will be worth it all just to see His

face, When He claims us for His own_____

_____ Then ten mil - lion years to sing a - maz - ing

grace; It will be worth it all when we get

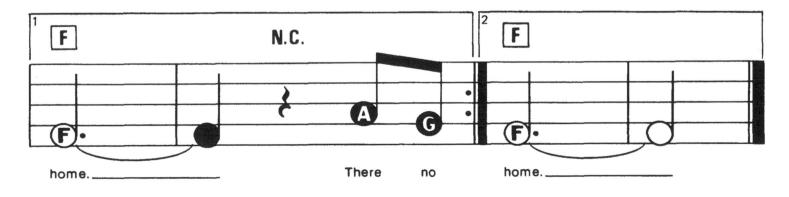

home._____ There no home._____

It's Beginning To Rain

Registration 3
Rhythm: Waltz

Words by Gloria Gaither and Aaron Wilburn
Music by William J. Gaither and Aaron Wilburn

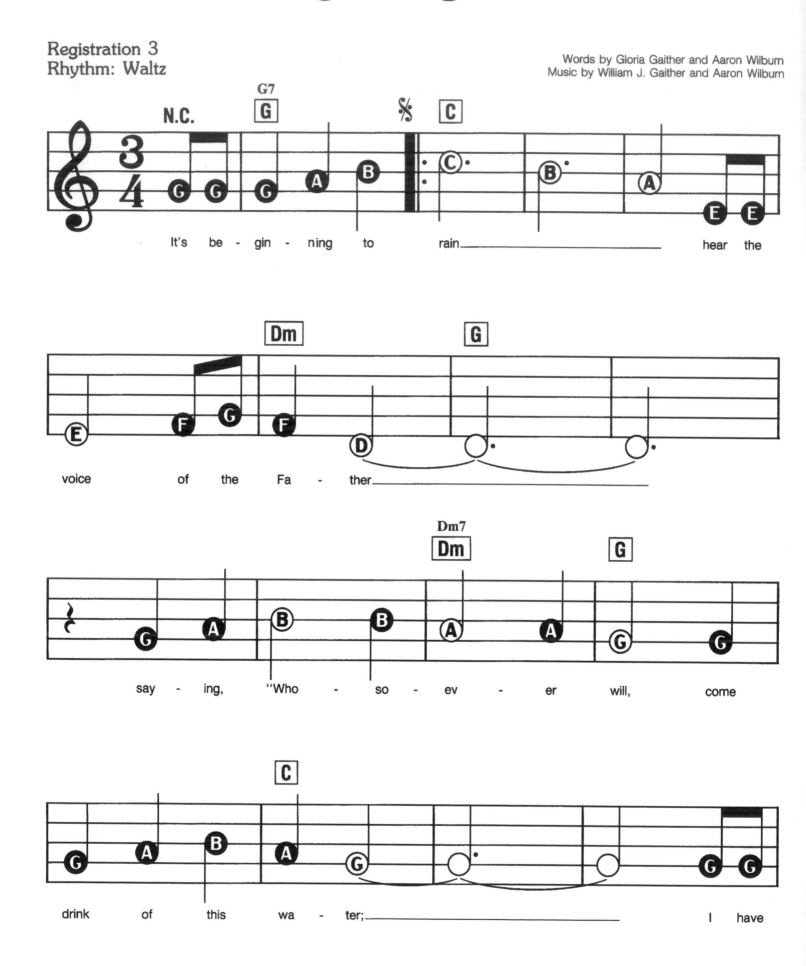

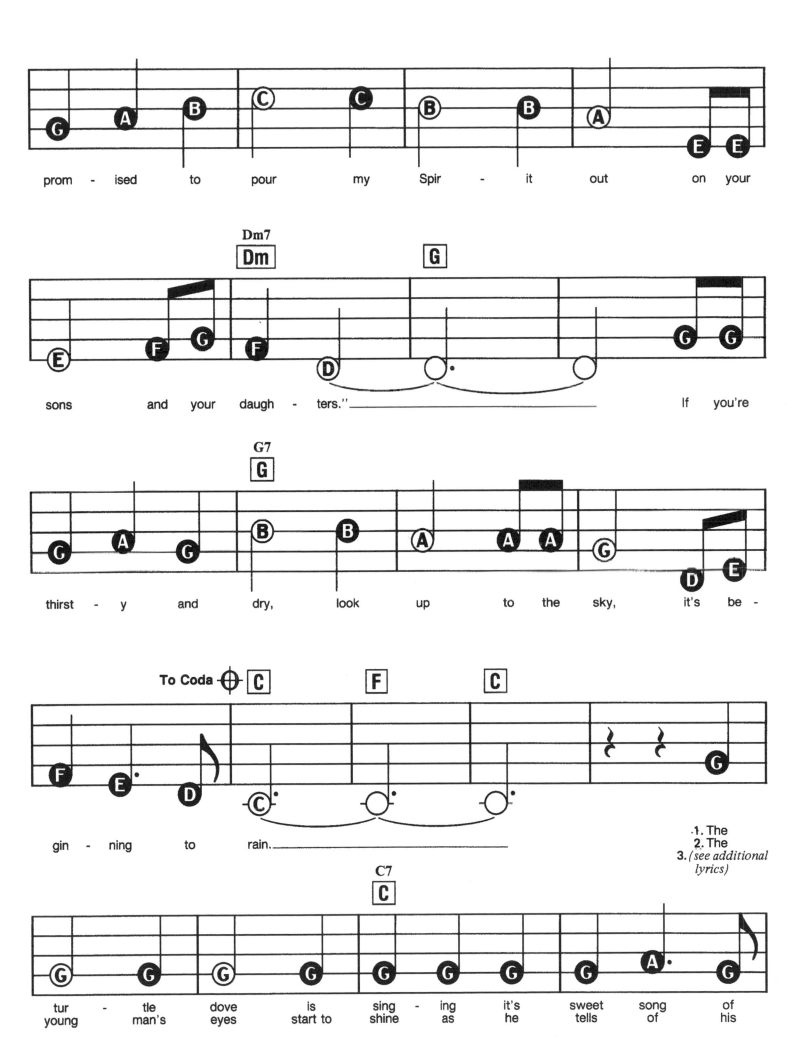

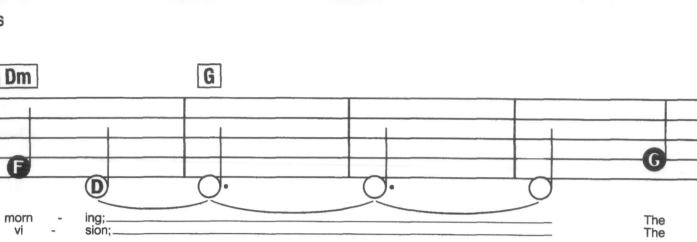

morn - ing; _____ The
vi - sion; _____ The

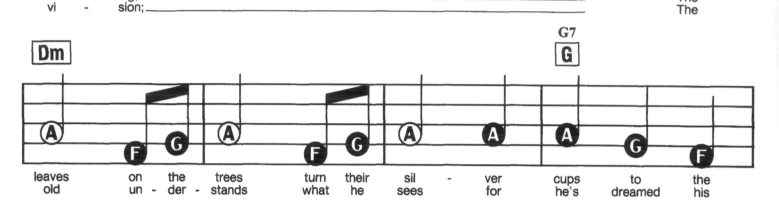

leaves   on the   trees   turn their   sil - ver   for   cups   to   the
old   un - der - stands   what he   sees   for   he's   dreamed his

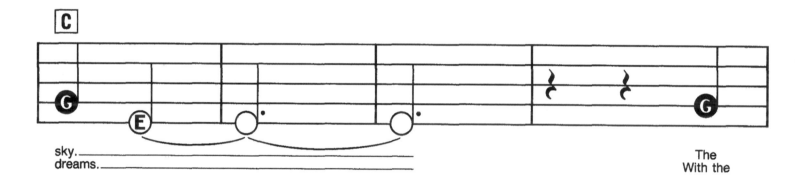

sky. _____ The
dreams. _____ With the

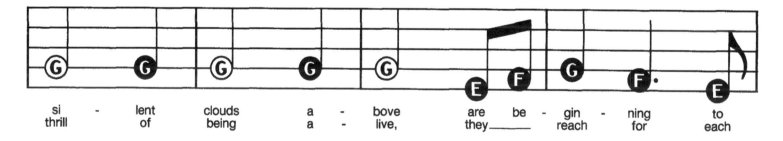

si - lent   clouds   a - bove   are be - gin - ning   to
thrill of   being   a - live,   they____ reach for   each

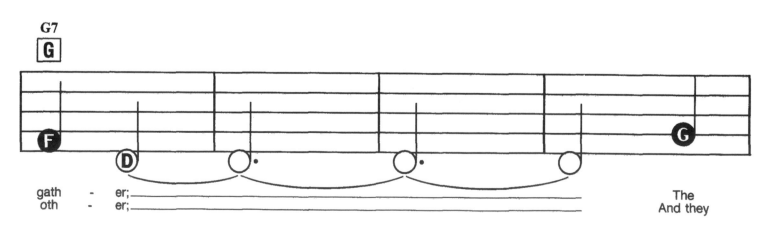

gath - er; _____ The
oth - er; _____ And they

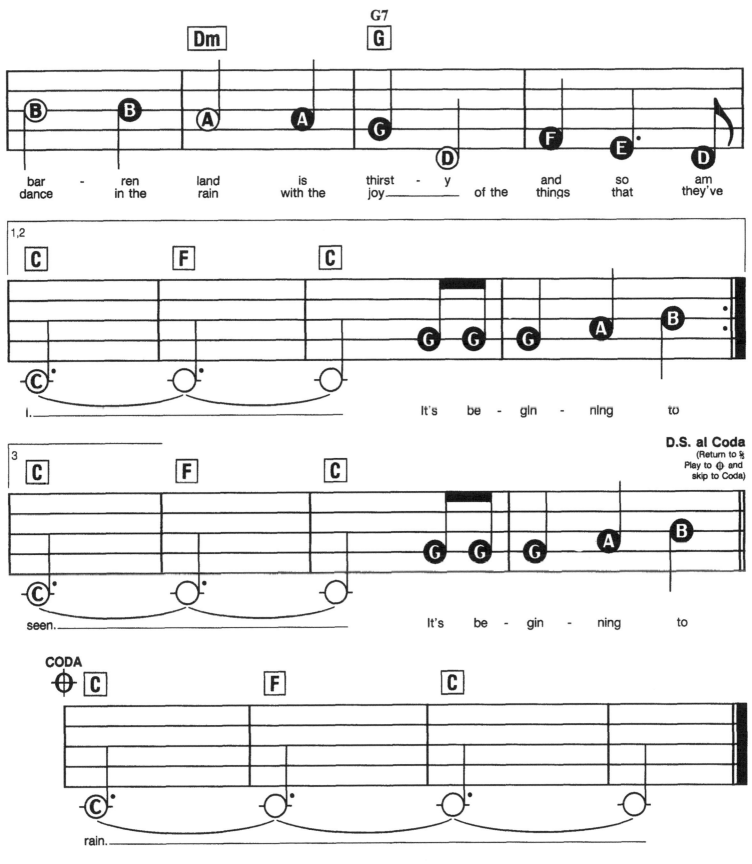

Additional Lyrics

3. At the first drop of rain that you hear, throw open the windows;
Go call all your children together and throw wide the door.
When the rains of the Spirit are falling, fill every vessel,
For he who drinks his fill will thirst no more.

Jesus Is Lord Of All

Registration 2
Rhythm: Waltz

Words by William J. & Gloria Gaither
Music by William J. Gaither

79

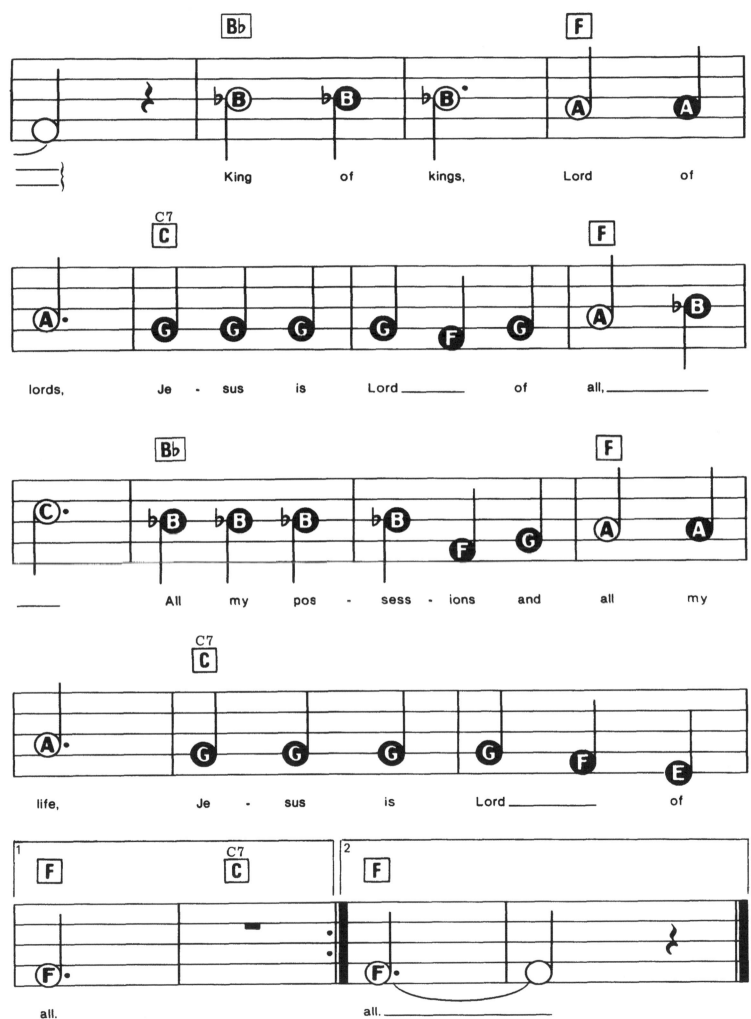

Jesus, I Believe What You Said

Registration 5
Rhythm: Rock or 8 Beat

Words by William J. & Gloria Gaither
Music by William J. Gaither

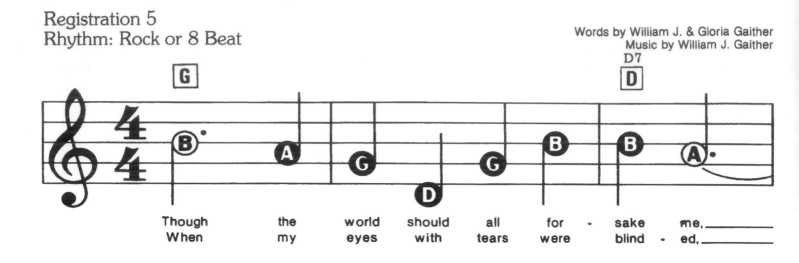

Though the world should all for - sake me,_____
When my eyes with tears were blind - ed,_____

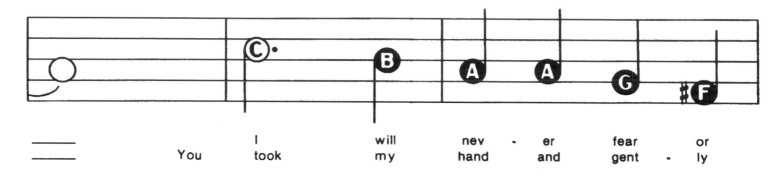

_____ You I took will my nev - er fear or
_____ You I took will my hand and gent - ly

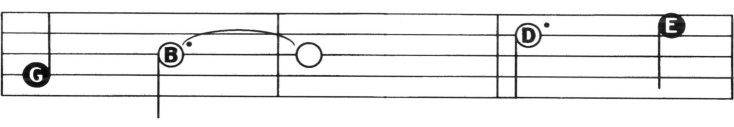

dread,_____ For You
led,_____ Oh, how

G7

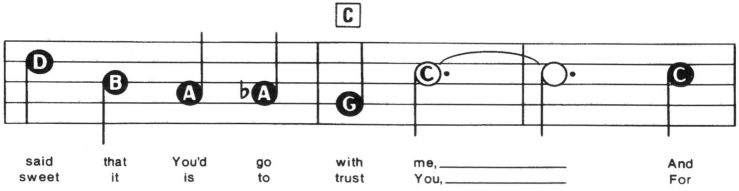

said that You'd go with me,_____ And
sweet it is to trust You,_____ For

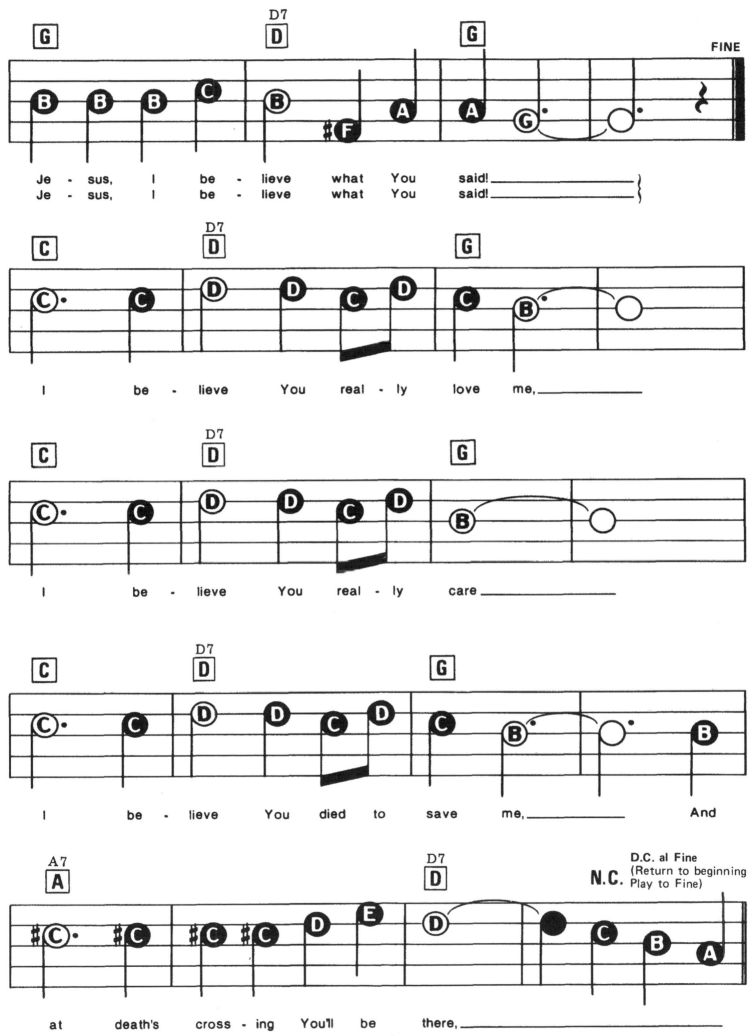

Jesus, I Heard You Had A Big House

Registration 3
Rhythm: Rock

Words by William J. & Gloria Gaither
Music by William J. Gaither

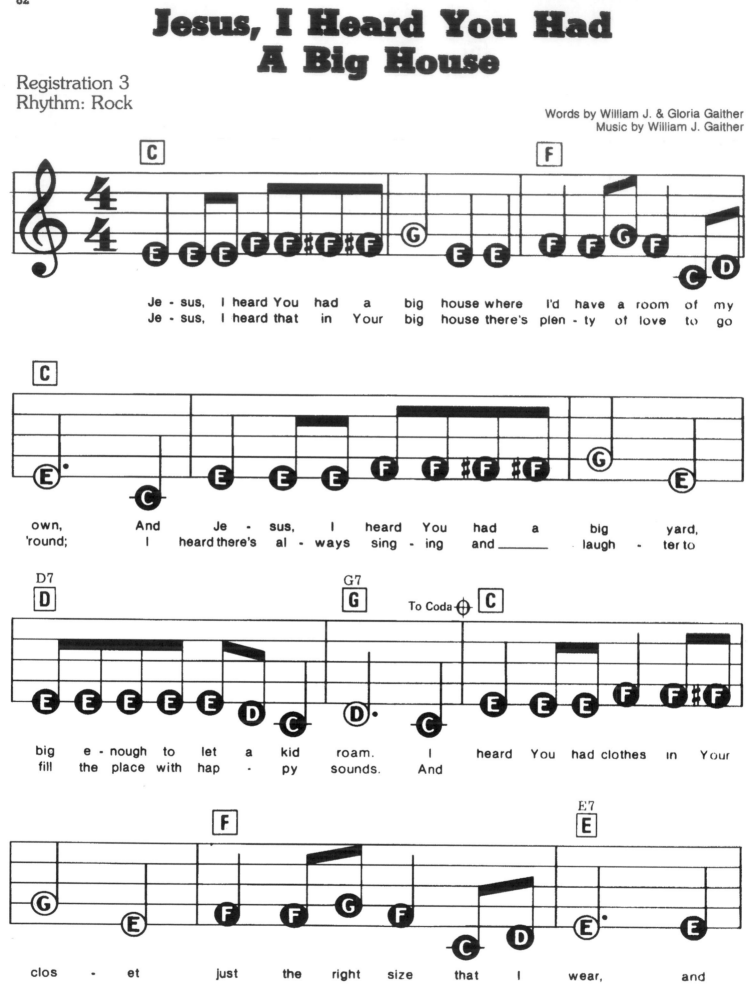

83

D.C. al Coda
(Return to beginning
Play to ⊕ and skip to Coda)

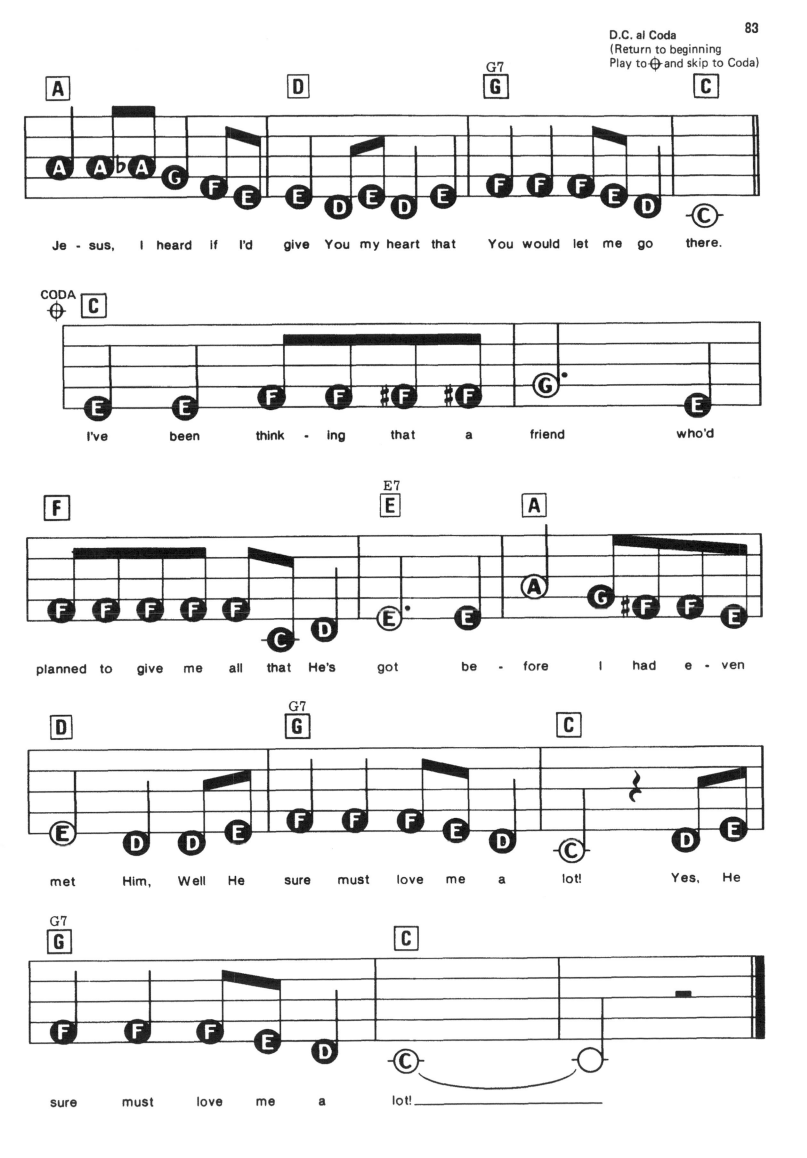

Je - sus, I heard if I'd give You my heart that You would let me go there.

CODA

I've been think - ing that a friend who'd

planned to give me all that He's got be - fore I had e - ven

met Him, Well He sure must love me a lot! Yes, He

sure must love me a lot! _____

Joy Comes In The Morning

Registration 2
Rhythm: 8 Beat or Pops

Words by William J. & Gloria Gaither
Music by William J. Gaither

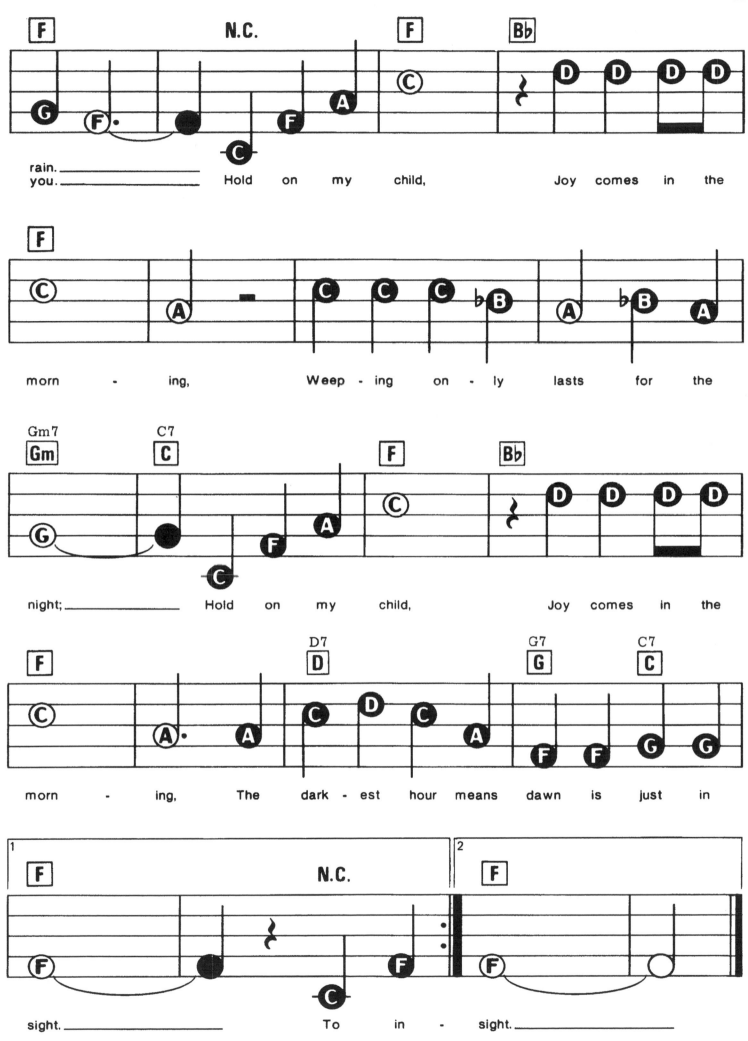

The King Is Coming

Registration 6
Rhythm: Waltz

Words by William J. & Gloria Gaither
and Charles Milhuff
Music by William J. Gaither

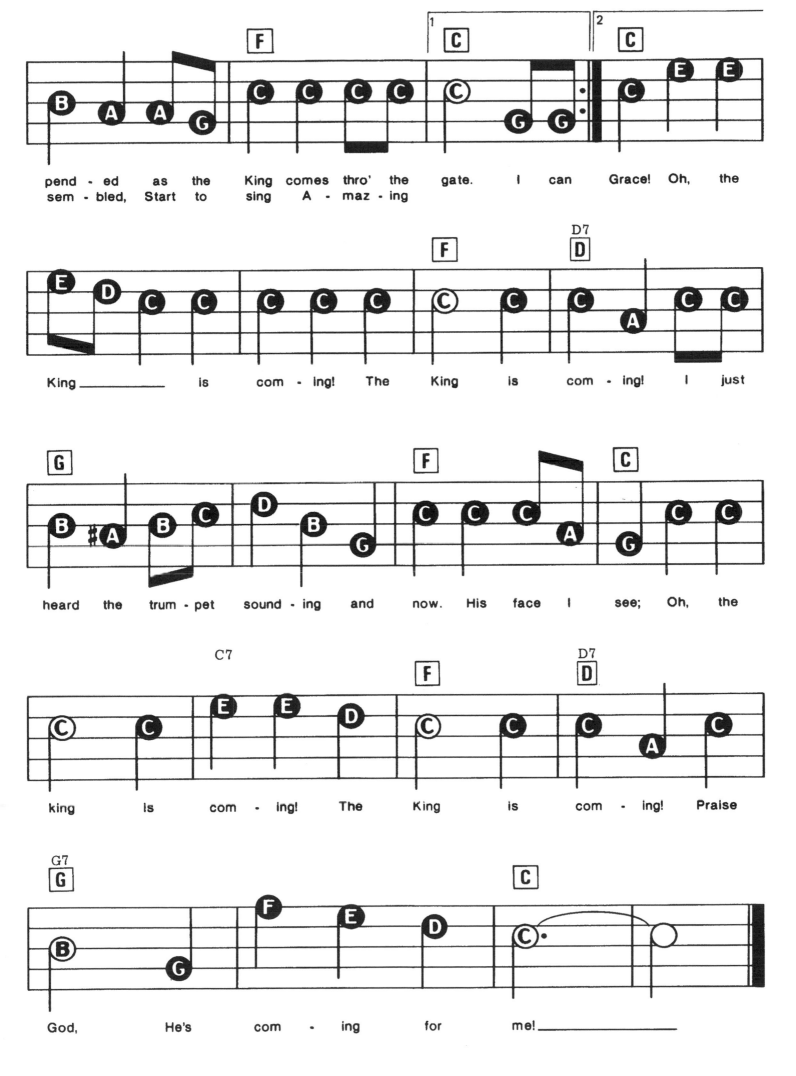

Learning To Live Like
A Child Of The King

Registration 5
Rhythm: Swing or Jazz

Words and Music by Gary S. Paxton
Gloria Gaither and William J. Gaither

89

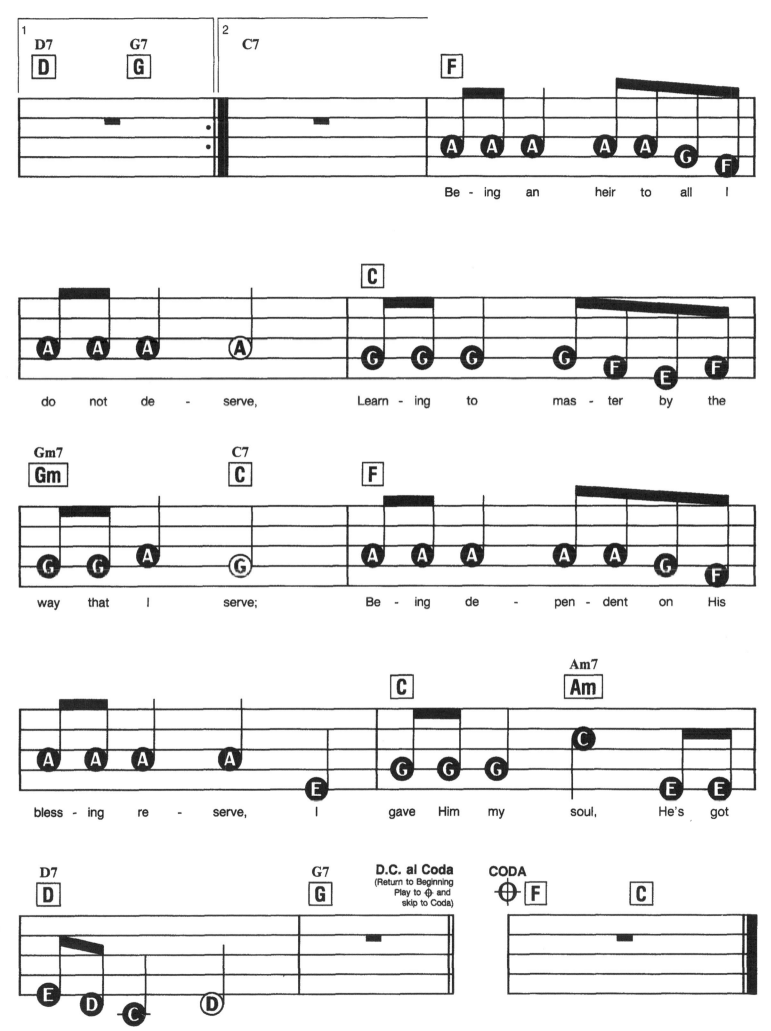

Let's Just Praise The Lord

Registration 4
Rhythm: Waltz

Words by William J. & Gloria Gaither
Music by William J. Gaither

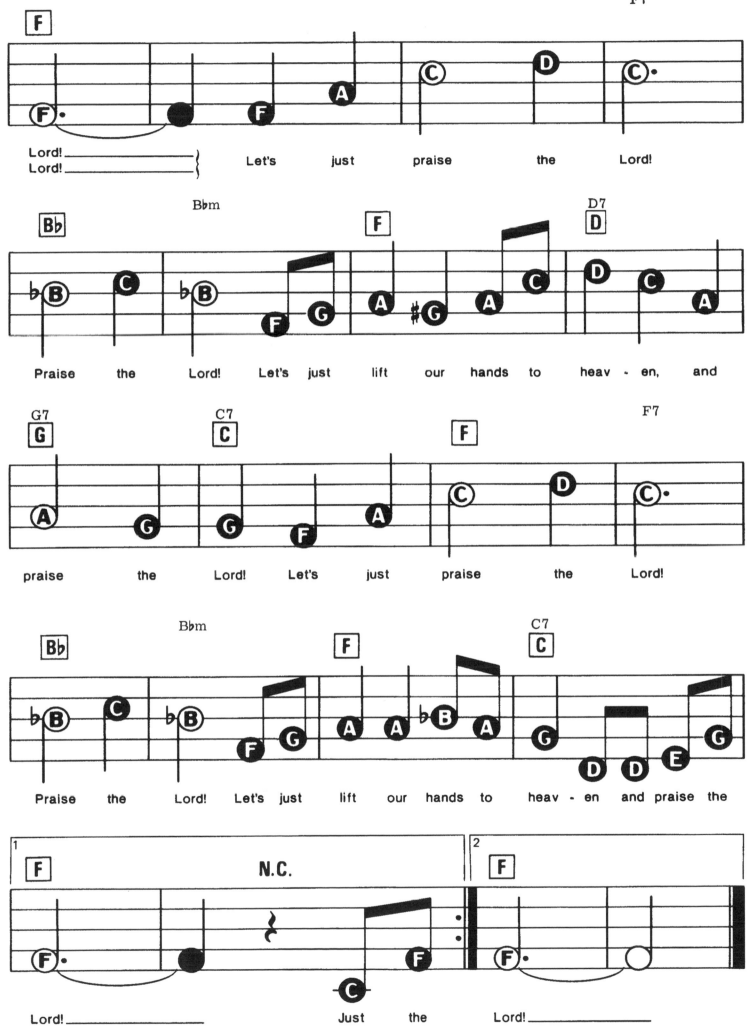

The Longer I Serve Him
(The Sweeter He Grows)

Registration 3
Rhythm: Waltz

Words and Music by
William J. Gaither

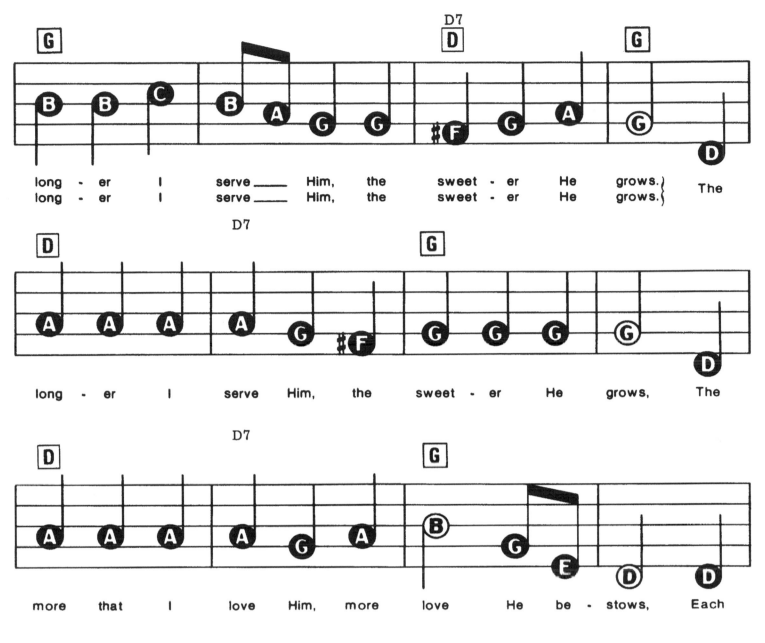

long - er I serve _____ Him, the sweet - er He grows.} The
long - er I serve _____ Him, the sweet - er He grows.}

long - er I serve Him, the sweet - er He grows, The

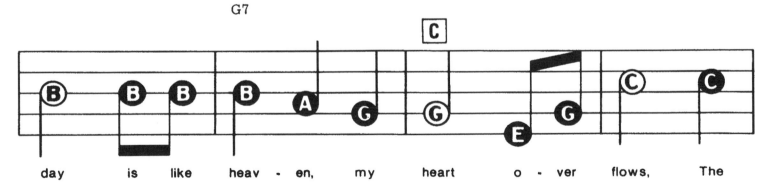

more that I love Him, more love He be - stows, Each

day is like heav - en, my heart o - ver flows, The

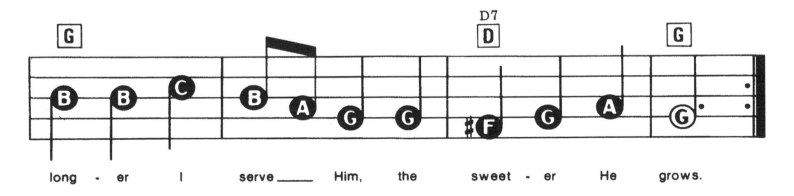

long - er I serve _____ Him, the sweet - er He grows.

Lovest Thou Me
(More Than These?)

Registration 2
Rhythm: Waltz

Words and Music by
William J. Gaither

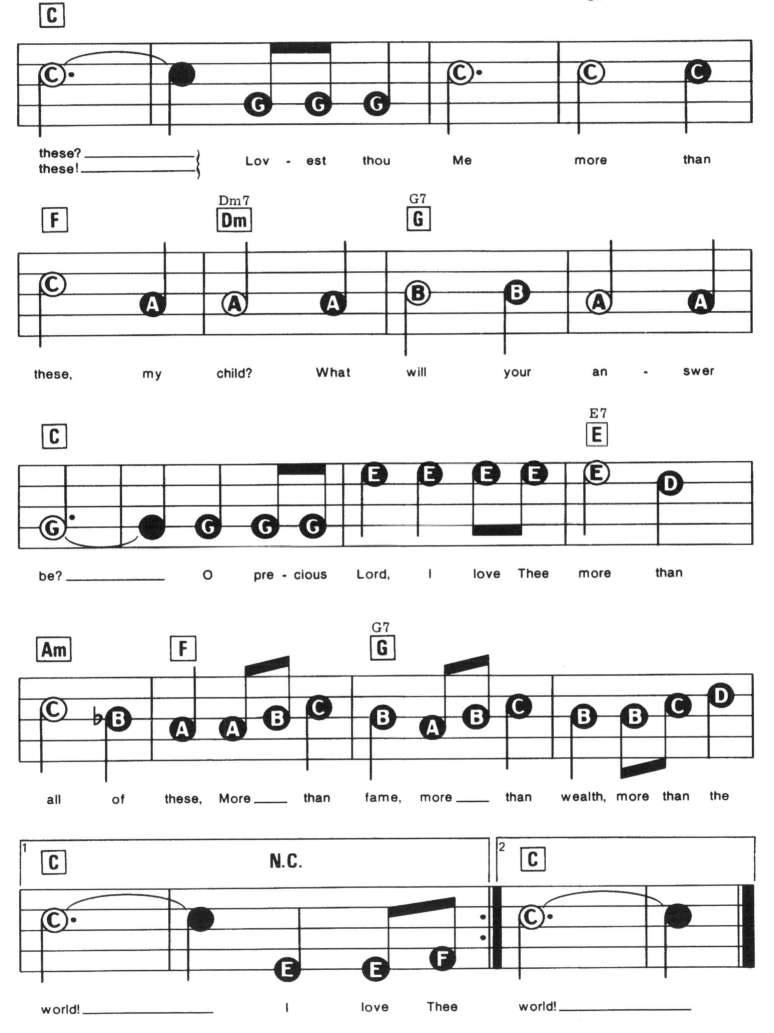

More Of You

Registration 4
Rhythm: Rock

Words by Gloria Gaither
Music by William J. Gaither and Gary S. Paxton

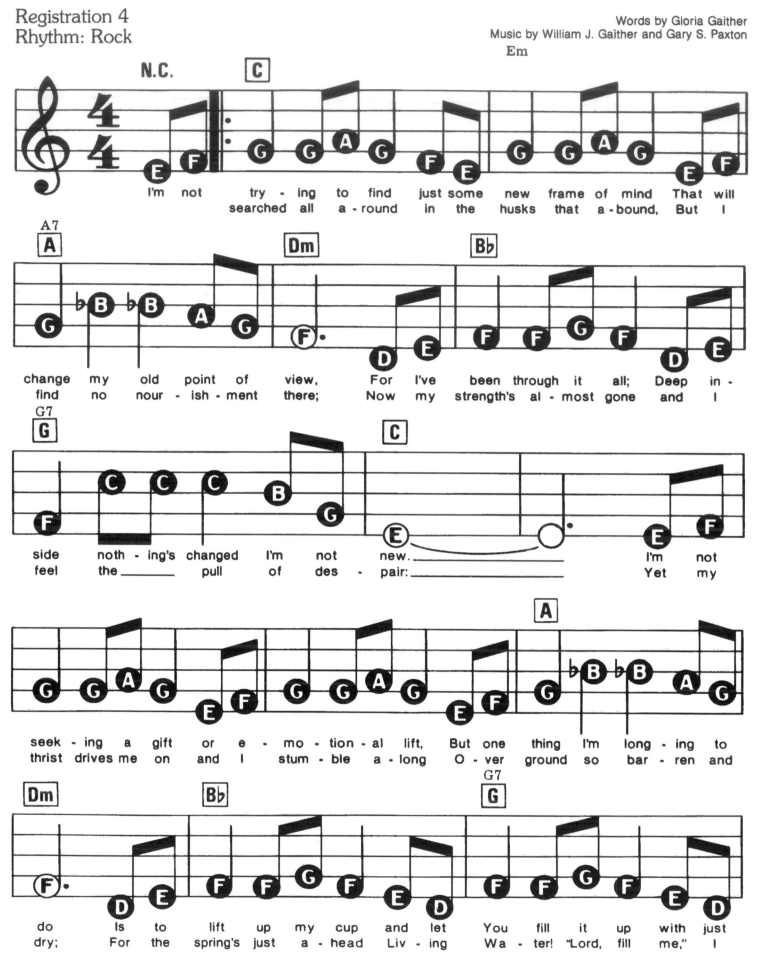

97

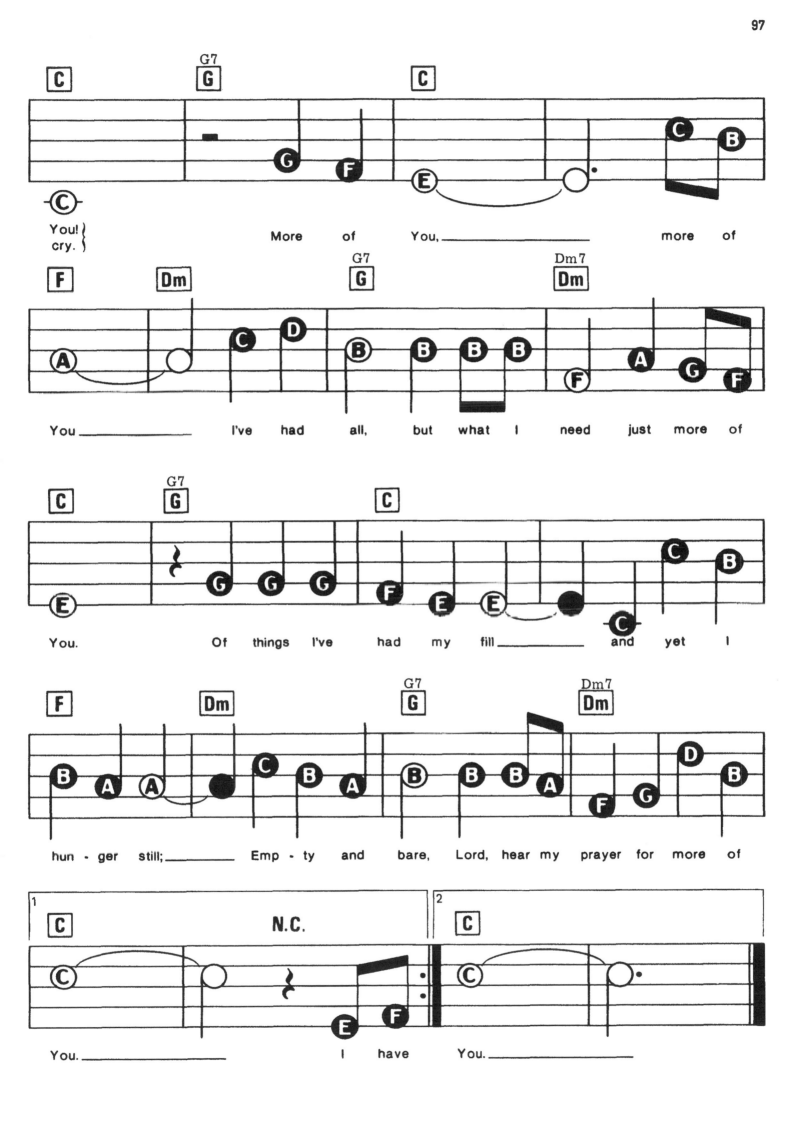

My Faith Still Holds

Registration 2
Rhythm: Swing

Words by William J. & Gloria Gaither
Music by William J. Gaither

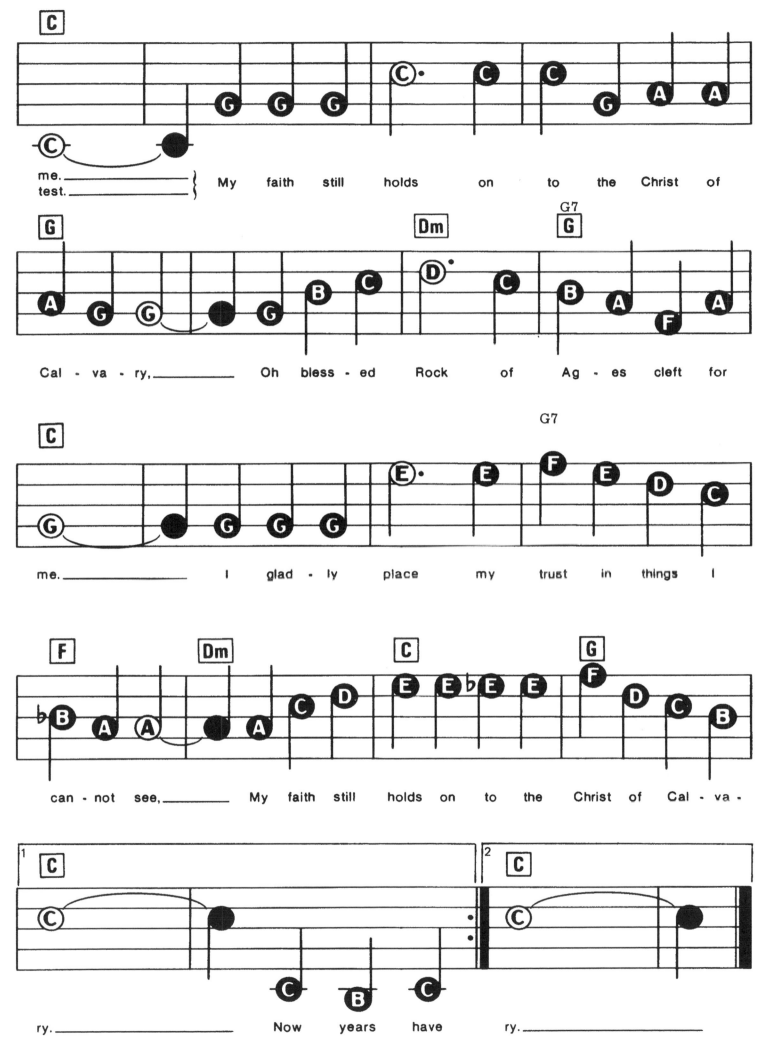

Man Can't Live By Bread Alone

Registration 6
Rhythm: Rock or 8 Beat

Words by Gloria Gaither
Music by William J. Gaither

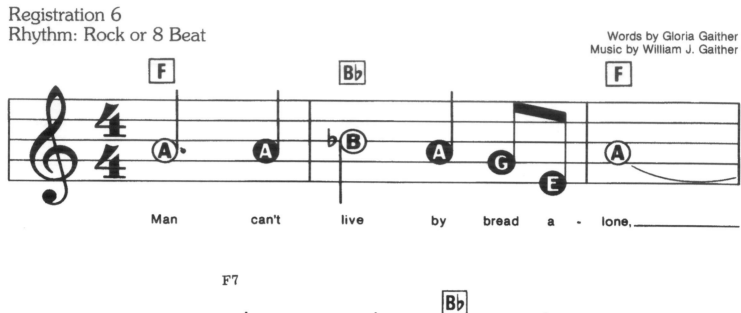

Man   can't   live   by   bread   a - lone, _____

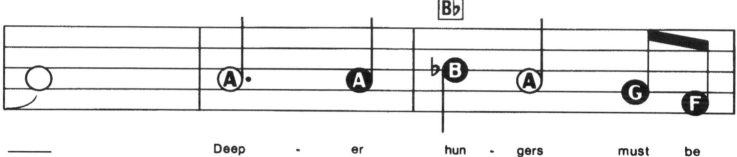

_____   Deep - er   hun - gers   must   be

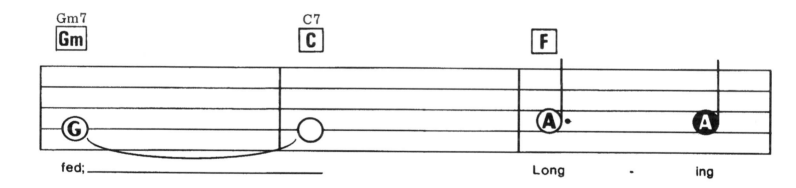

fed; _____   Long - ing

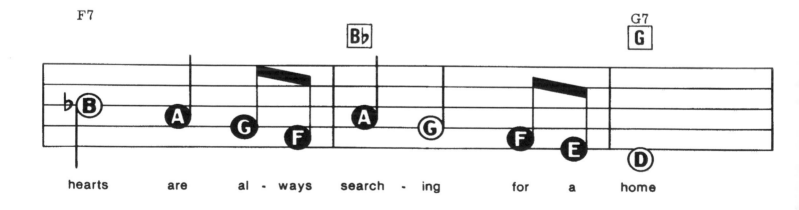

hearts   are   al - ways   search - ing   for   a   home

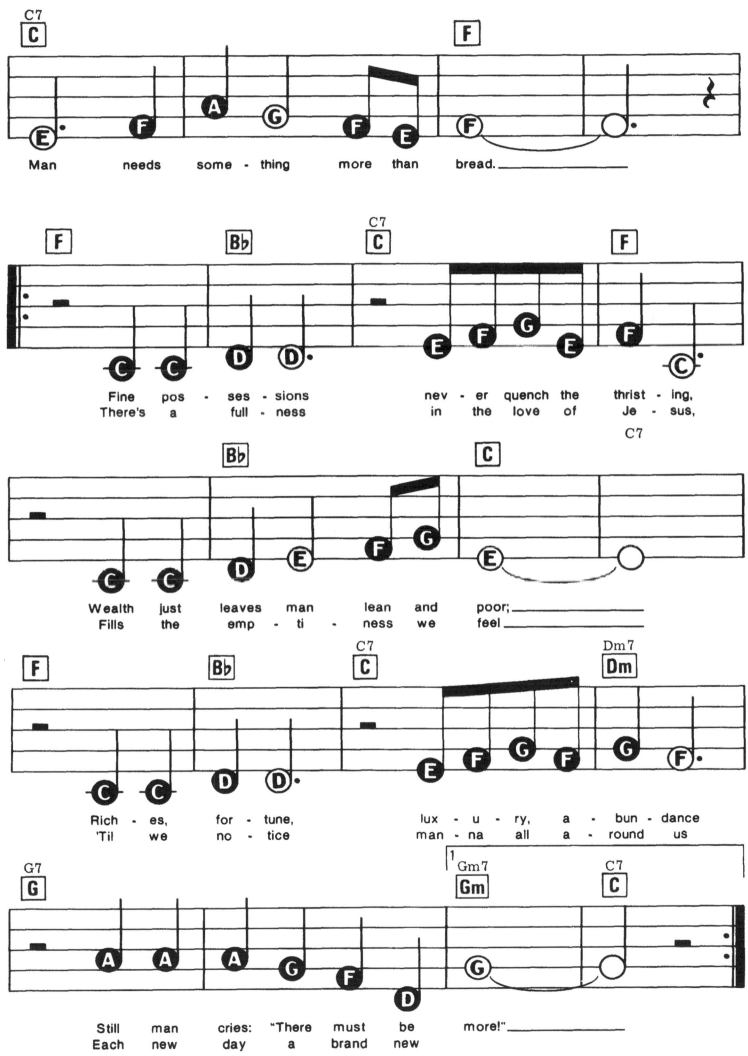

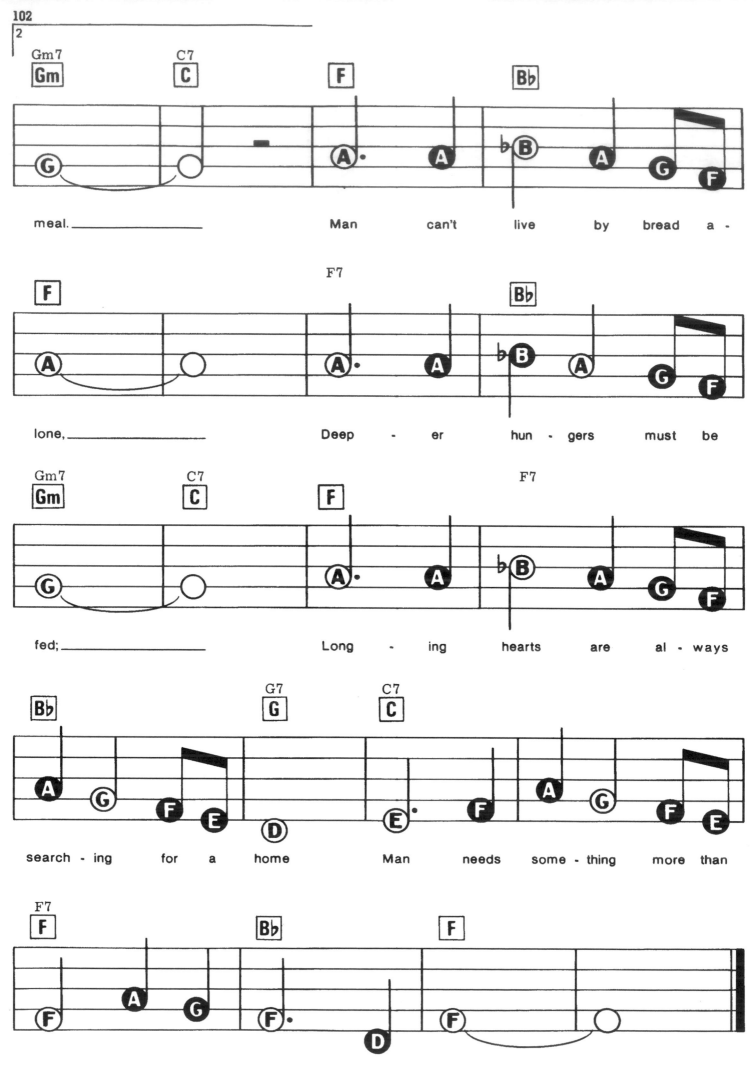

Next Time We Meet

Registration 3
Rhythm: Waltz

Words by Gloria Gaither
Music by William J. Gaither and Chris Waters

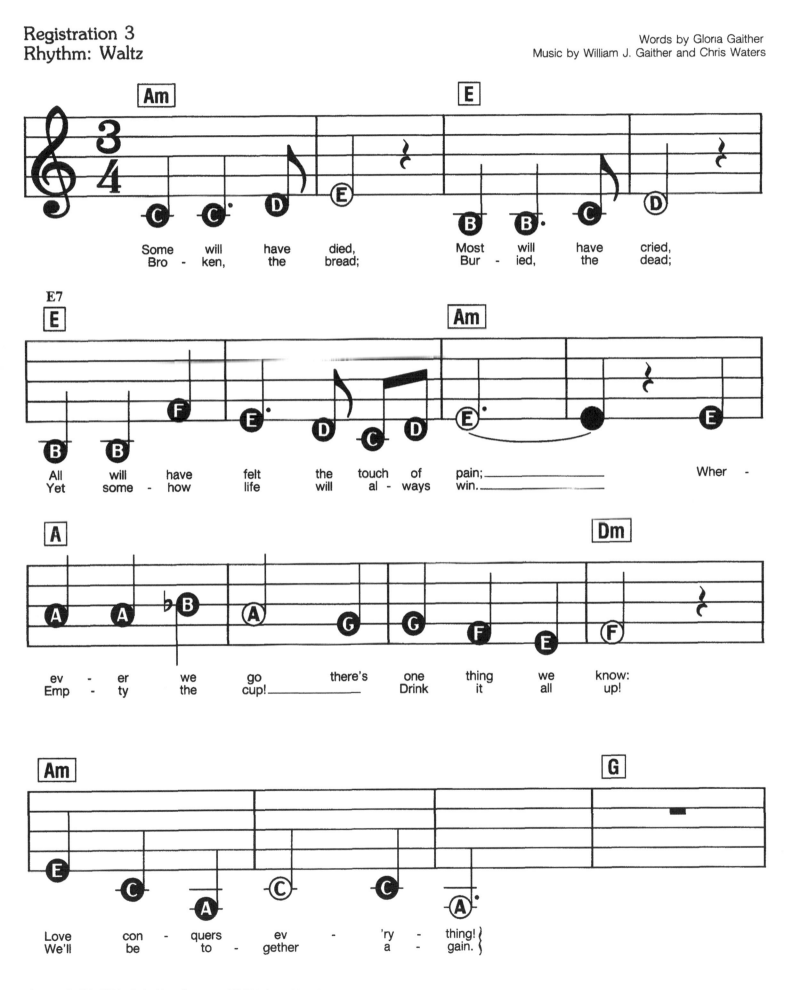

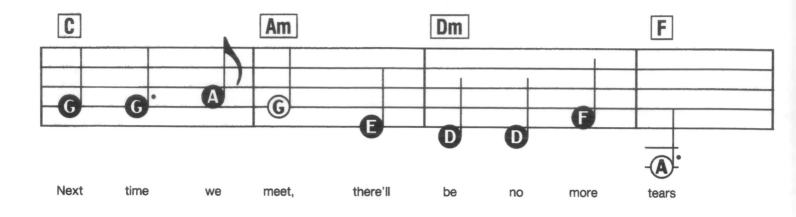

Next time we meet, there'll be no more tears

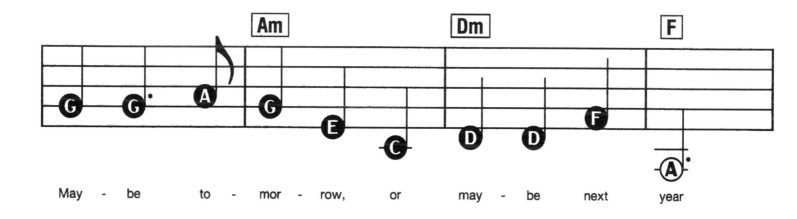

Next time we share the bread and the wine,

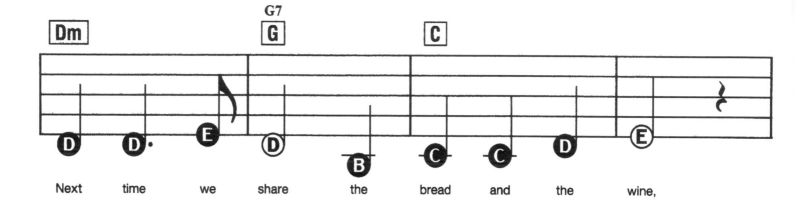

May - be to - mor - row, or may - be next year

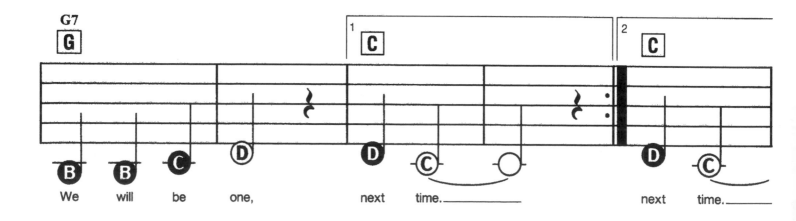

We will be one, next time._____ next time._____

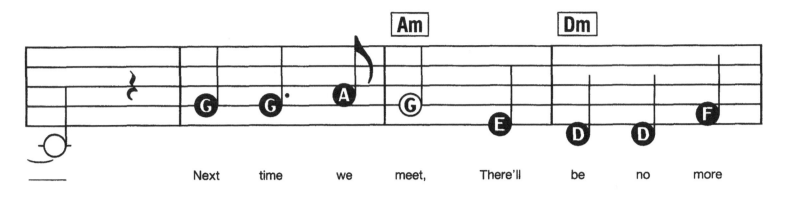

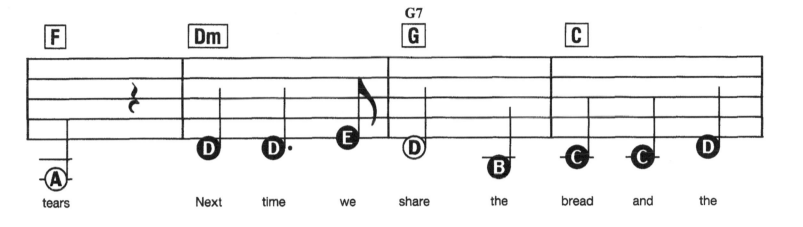

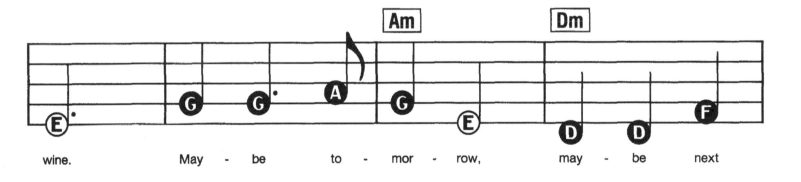

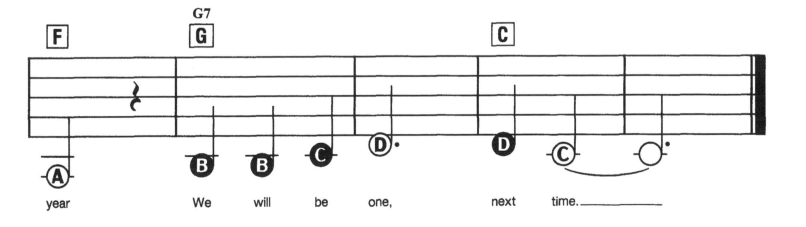

Not By Might, Not By Power

Registration: 4
Rhythm: Rock or Jazz Rock

Words by Gloria Gaither
Music by William J. Gaither and Chris Christian

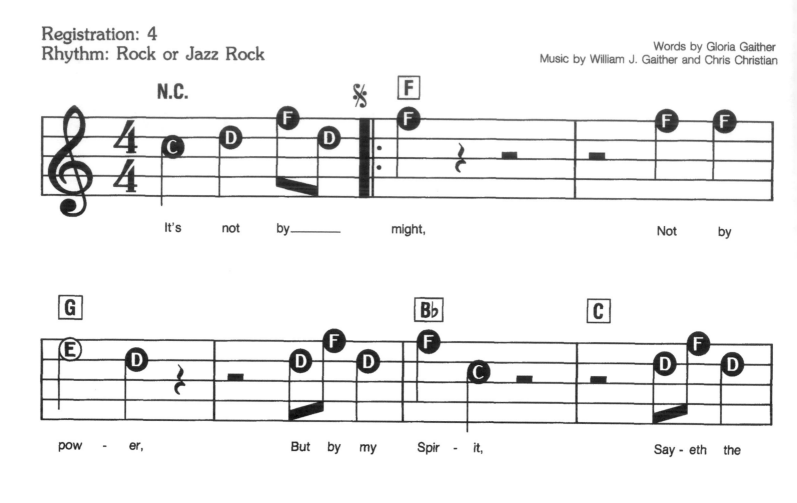

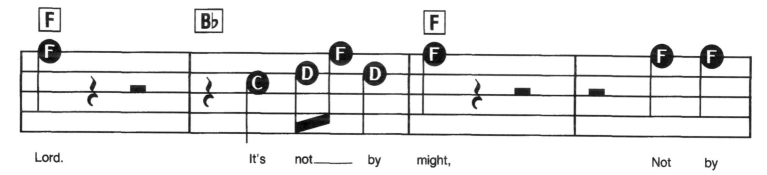

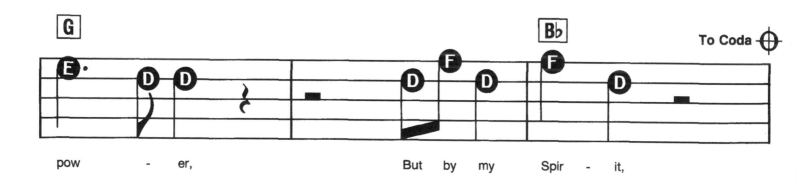

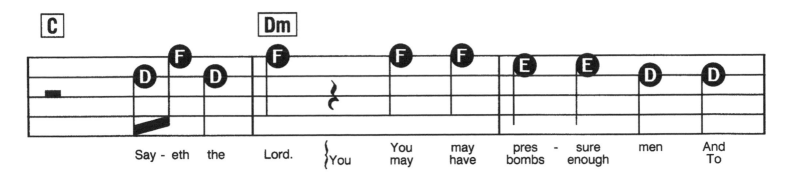

Say - eth the Lord. {You You may have pres - sure men And
bombs enough To

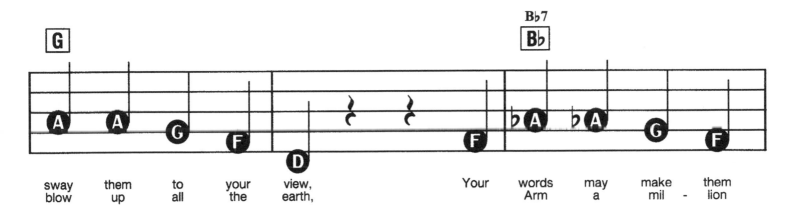

sway them to your view, Your words may make them
blow up all the earth, Arm a mil - lion

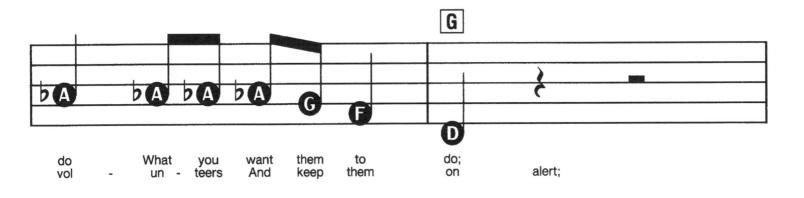

do - What you want them to do;
vol - un - teers And keep them on alert;

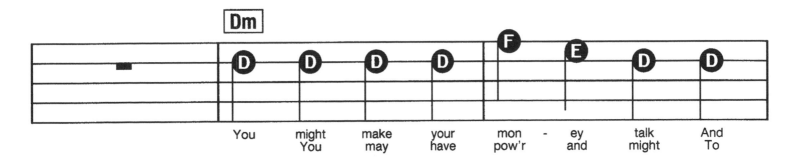

You might make your mon - ey talk And
You may have pow'r and might To

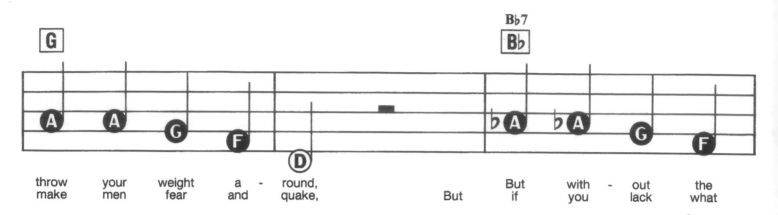

throw your weight a - round,
make your men fear and quake,
But But if with - out the what
you lack

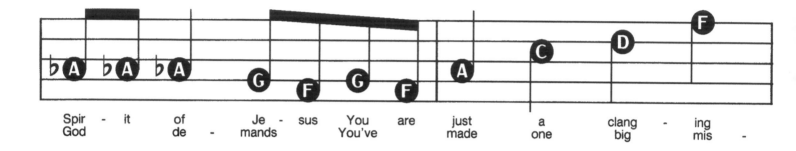

Spir - it of Je - sus You are just a clang - ing
God de - mands You've made one big mis -

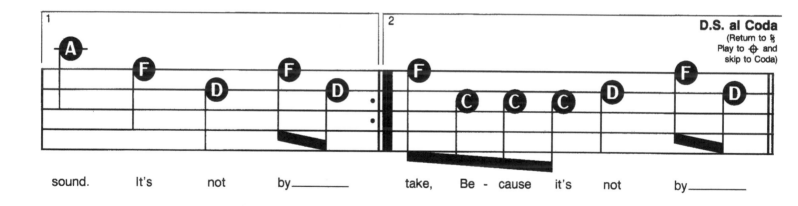

D.S. al Coda
(Return to %
Play to ⊕ and
skip to Coda)

sound. It's not by_____
take, Be - cause it's not by_____

CODA **C**

F

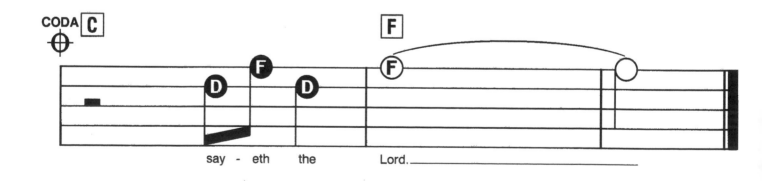

say - eth the Lord._____

Plenty Of Room In The Family

Registration 4
Rhythm: Rock

Words by William J. & Gloria Gaither
Music by William J. Gaither

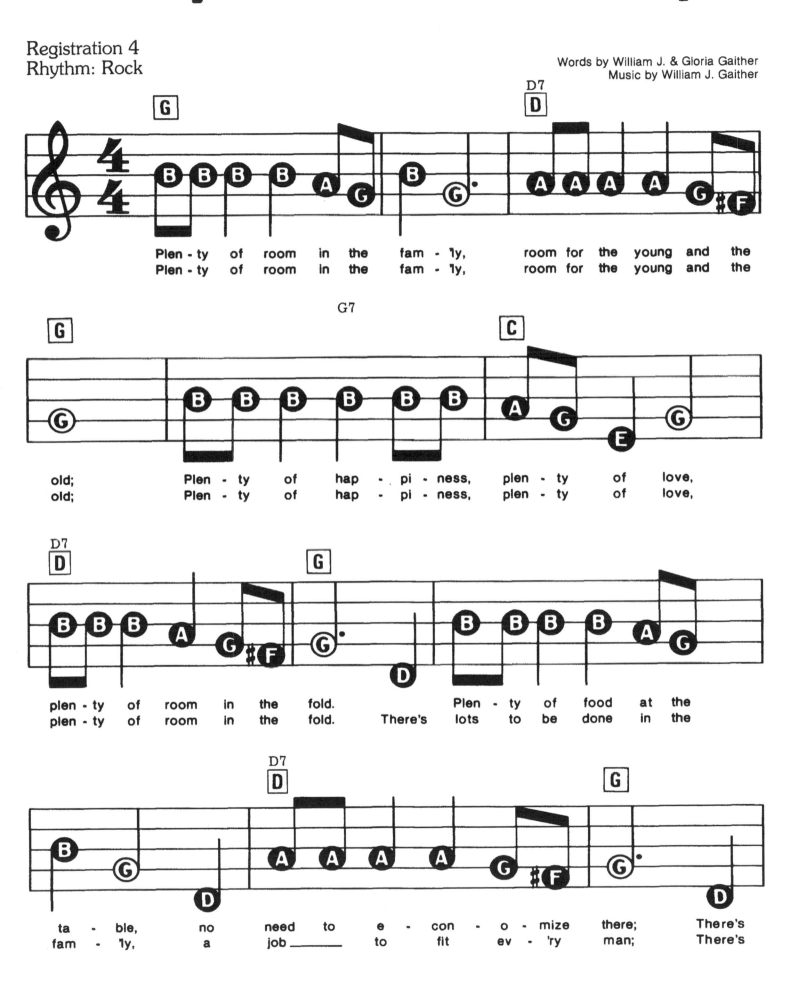

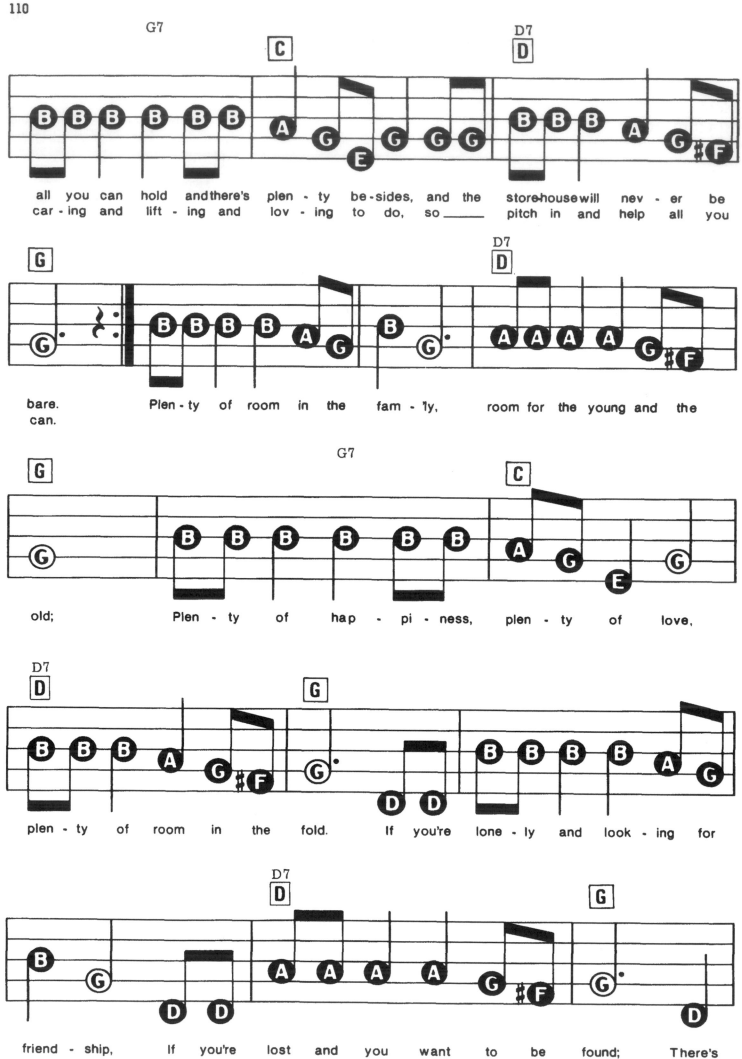

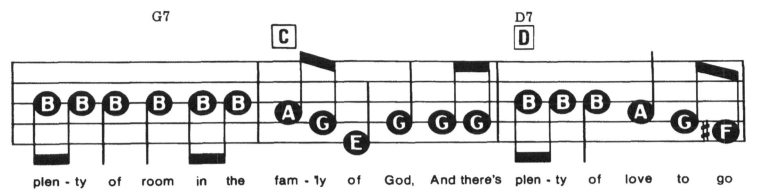

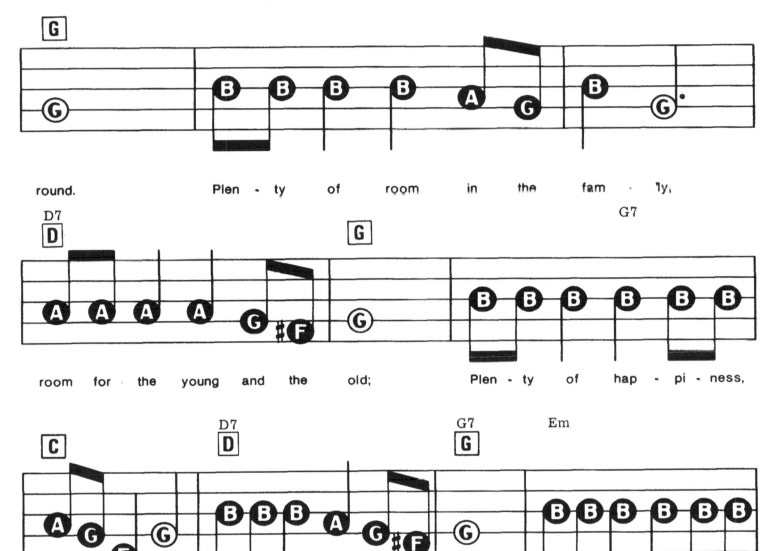

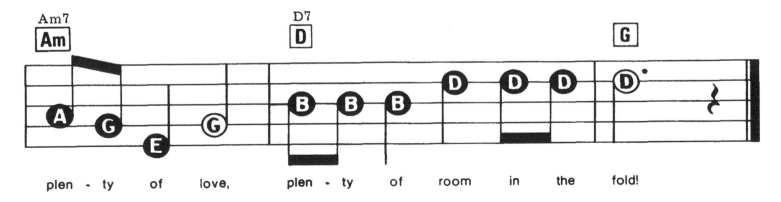

The Old Rugged Cross
Made The Difference

Registration 3
Rhythm: Waltz

Words by William J. & Gloria Gaither
Music by William J. Gaither

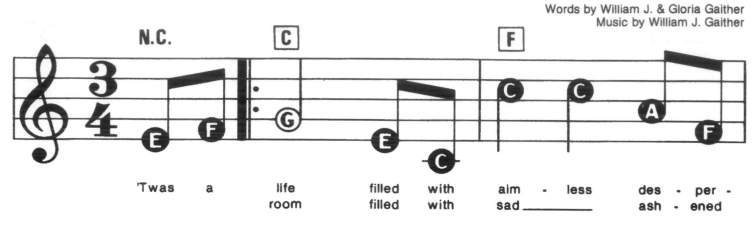

'Twas a life filled with aim - less des - per -
room filled with sad _____ ash - ened

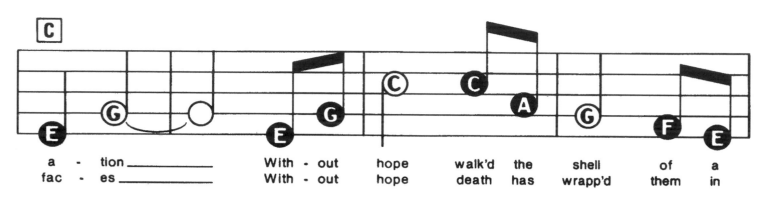

a - tion _____ With - out hope walk'd the shell of a
fac - es _____ With - out hope death has wrapp'd of them in

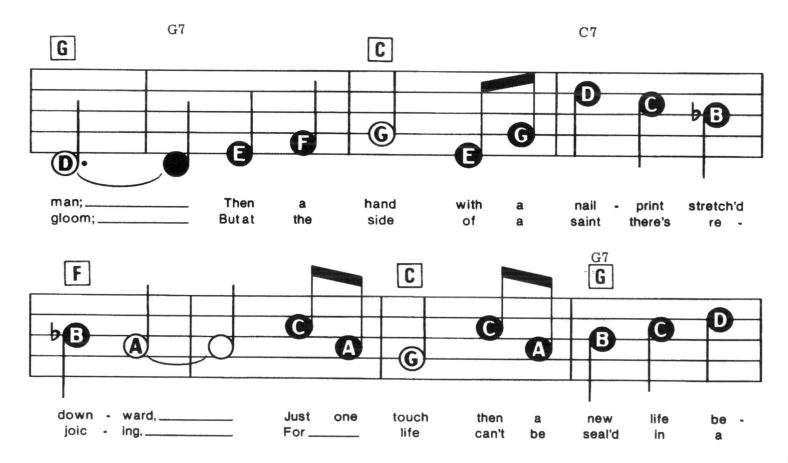

man; _____ Then a hand with a nail - print stretch'd
gloom; _____ But at the side of a saint there's re -

down - ward, _____ Just one touch then a new life be -
joic - ing. _____ For _____ life can't be seal'd in a

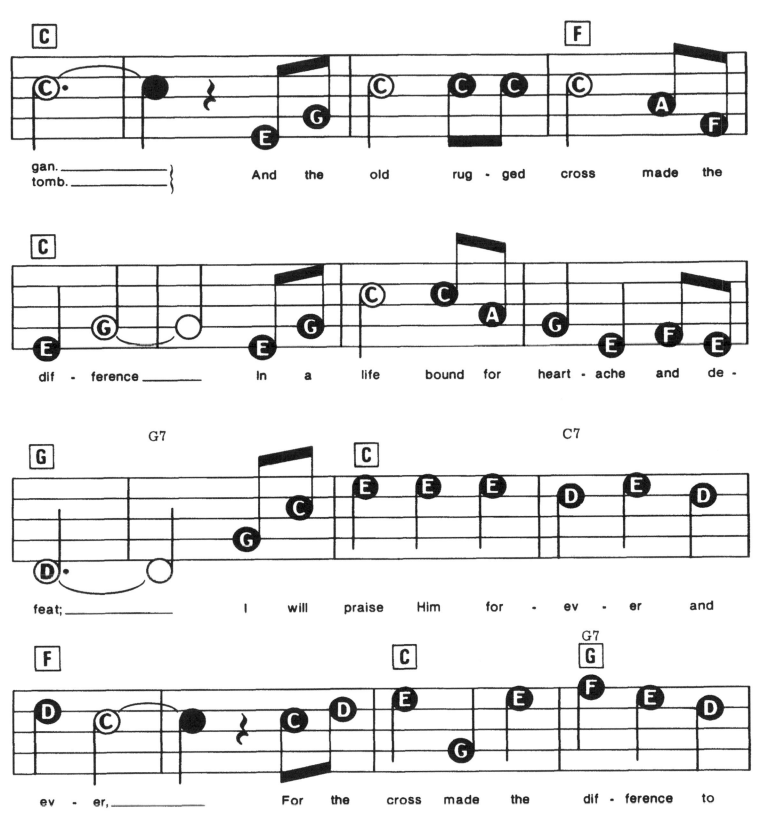

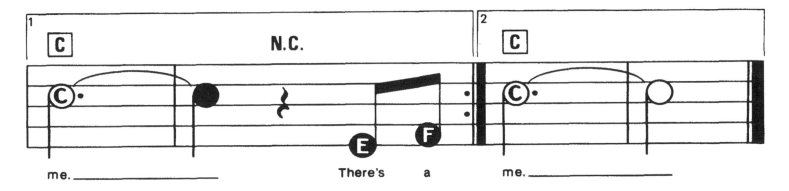

Precious Jesus

Registration 3
Rhythm: Rock or 8 Beat

Words by Jim Hill and Gloria Gaither
Music by Jim Hill

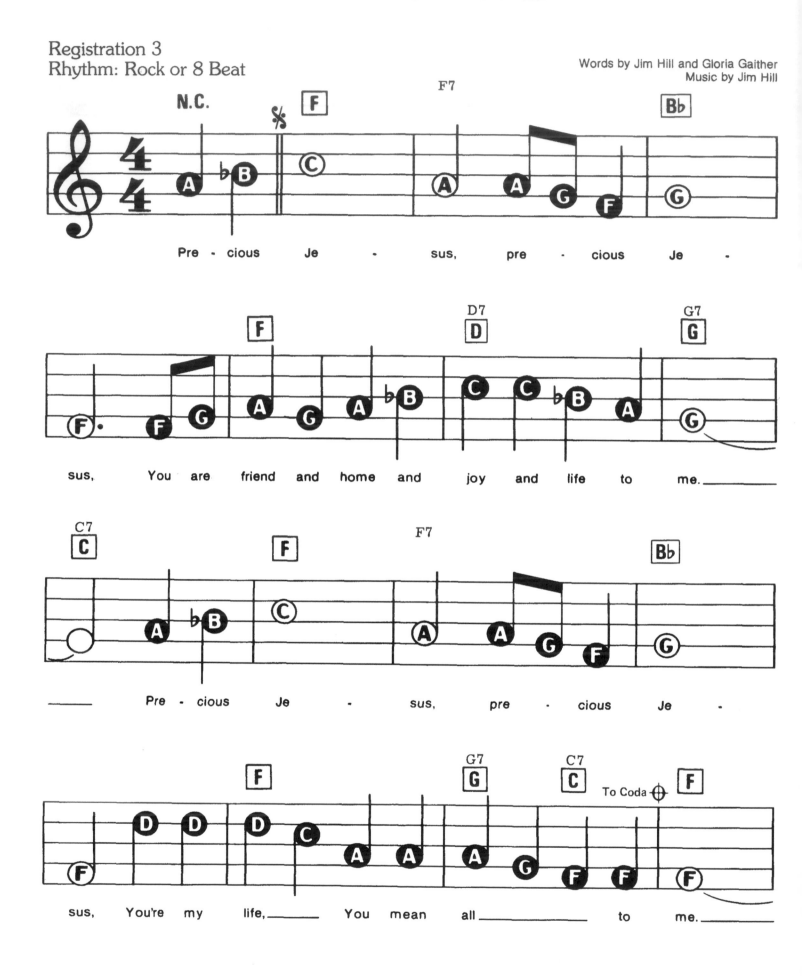

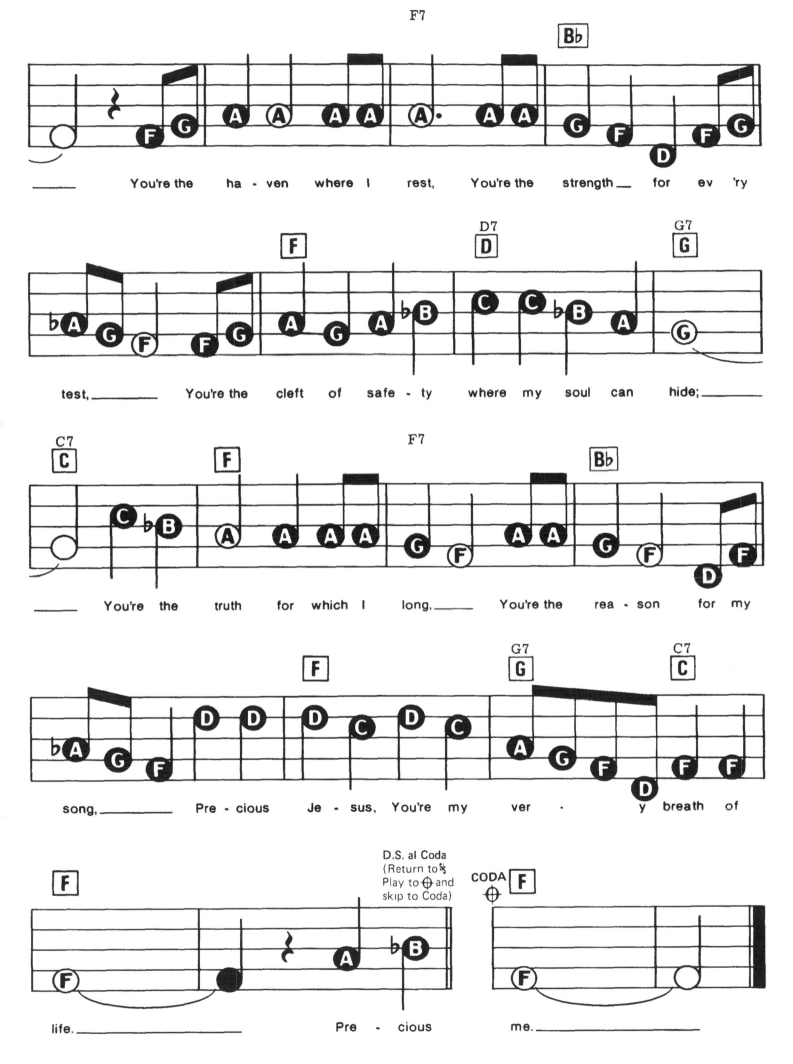

Redeeming Love

Registration 6
Rhythm: Swing

Words by Gloria Gaither
Music by William J. Gaither

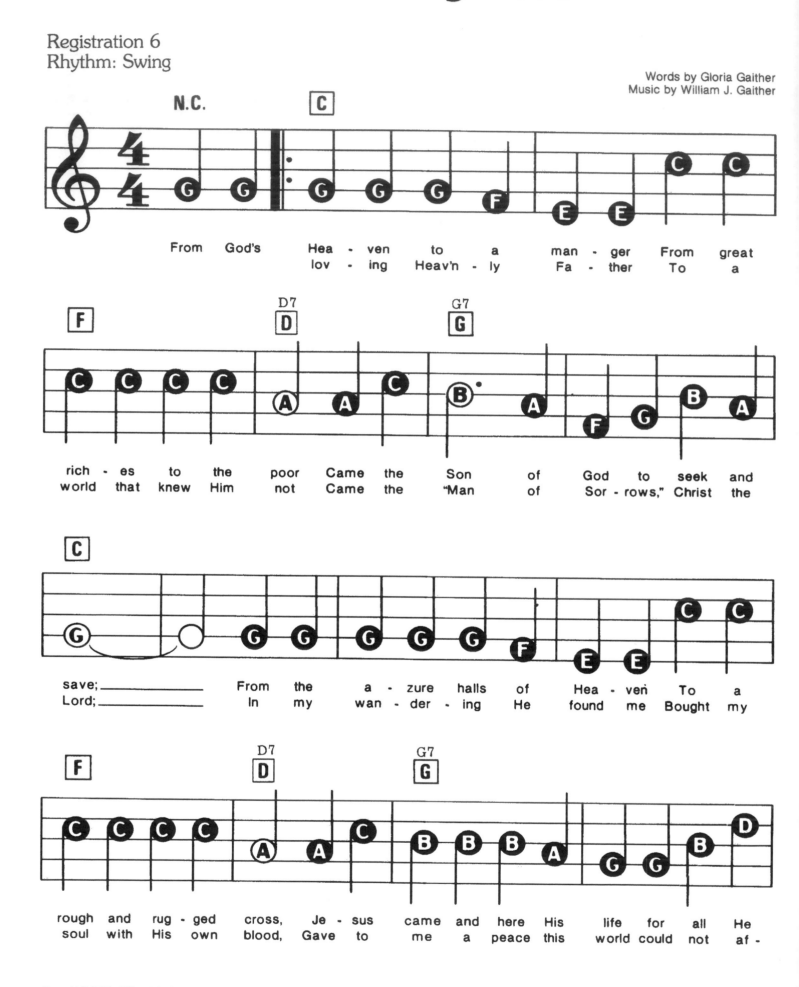

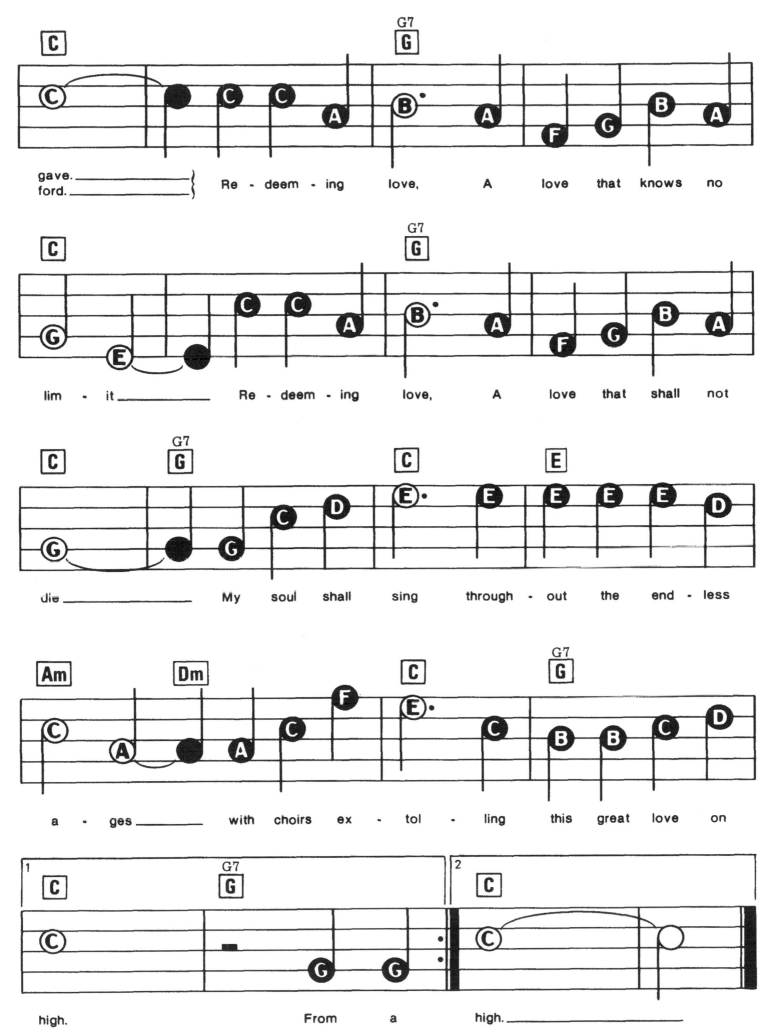

Reaching

Registration 2
Rhythm: 8 Beat or Pops

Words by William J. & Gloria Gaither
Music by William J. Gaither

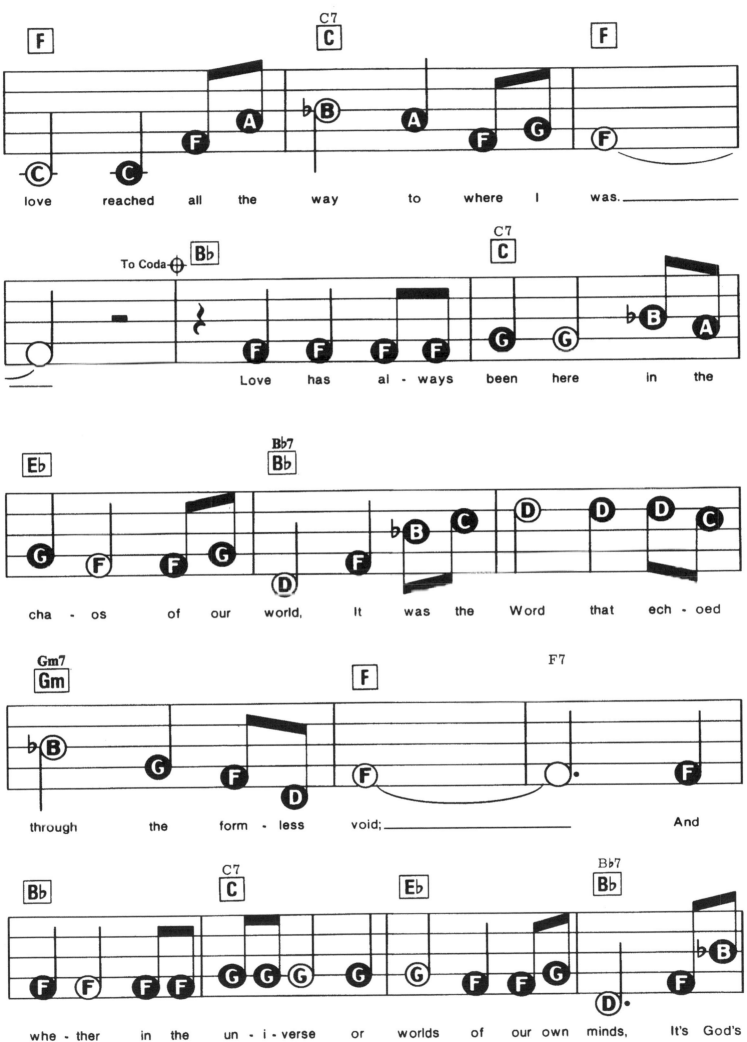

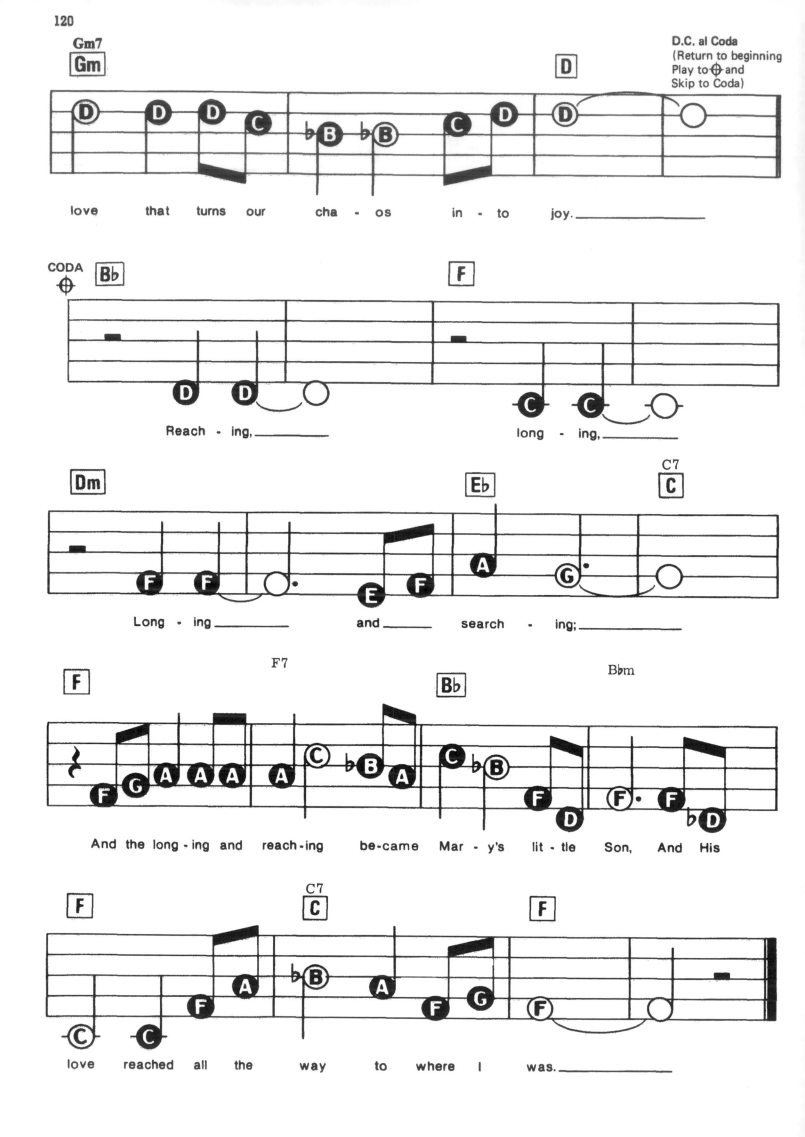

Tell It To Your Children

Registration 4
Rhythm: Rock

Words by William J. & Gloria Gaither
Music by William J. Gaither

Tell it to your chil - dren and your chil - dren's chil - dren,
Tell it to your chil - dren and your chil - dren's chil - dren,

Stamp it on the doors of their hearts; Make it a theme of the
Keep it right be - fore their eyes; Make it a pat - tern for

song that you sing, And sing it to them right from the start.
all that you do And the an - swer for all of their "whys".

Tell it in the morn - ing, tell it in the night
Whis - per when you're near, shout it from a - far;

Make it your life your
Make it what you live you've got to

122

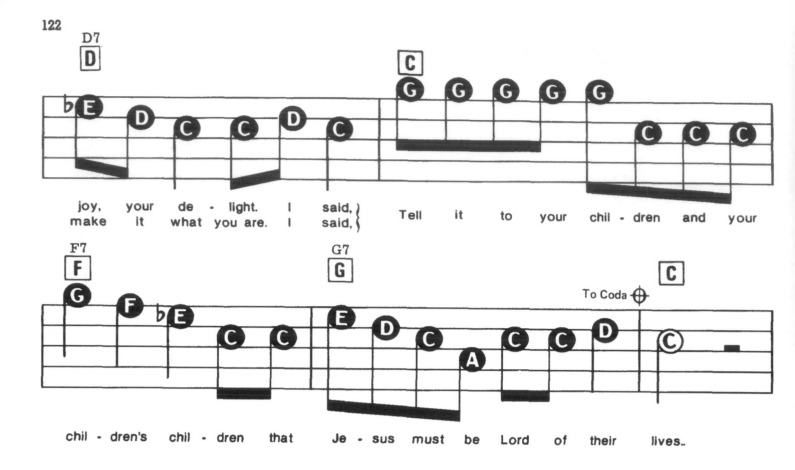

joy, your de-light. I said,}
make it what you are. I said,} Tell it to your chil-dren and your

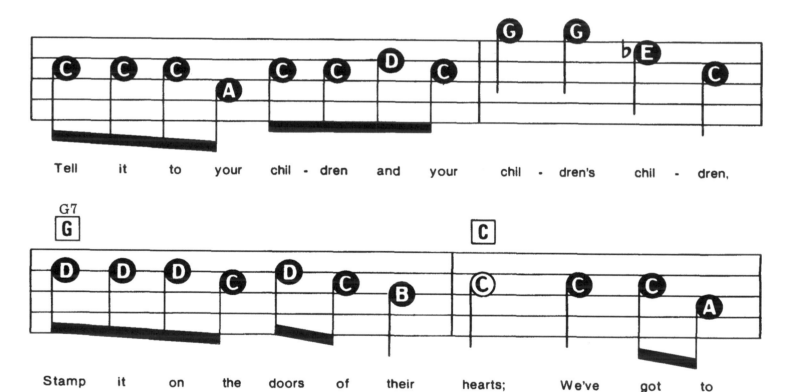

chil-dren's chil-dren that Je-sus must be Lord of their lives.

Tell it to your chil-dren and your chil-dren's chil-dren,

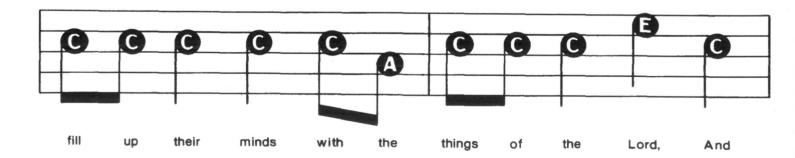

Stamp it on the doors of their hearts; We've got to

fill up their minds with the things of the Lord, And

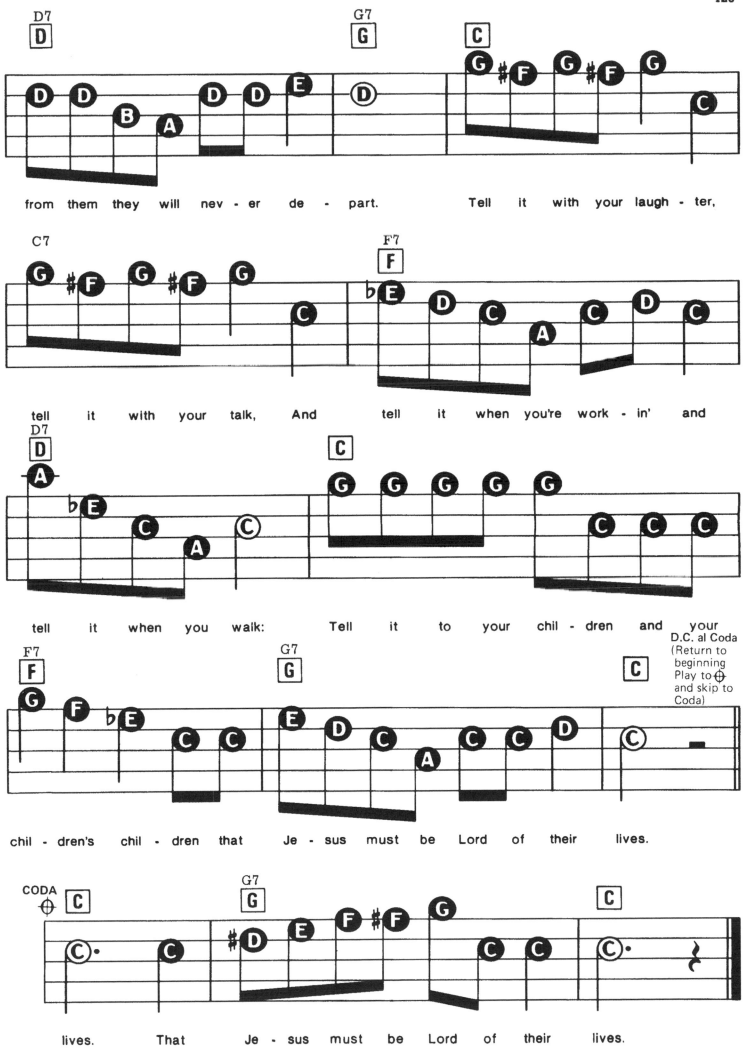

Something Beautiful

Registration 3
Rhythm: Swing

Words by Gloria Gaither
Music by William J. Gaither

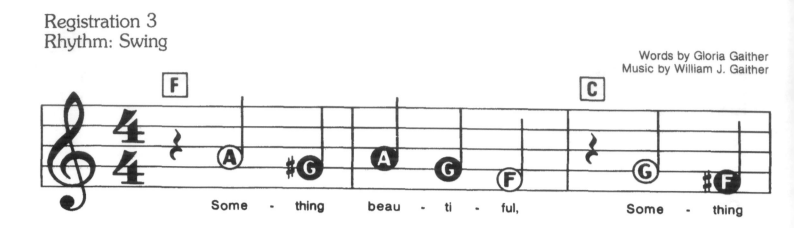

Some - thing beau - ti - ful, Some - thing

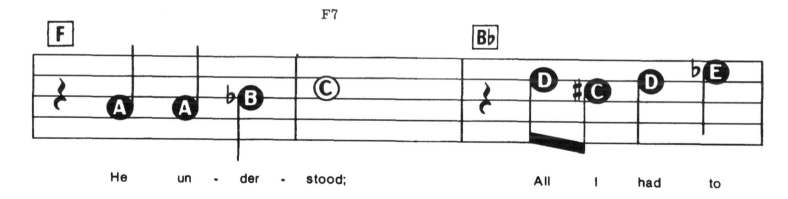

good; All my con - fu - sion

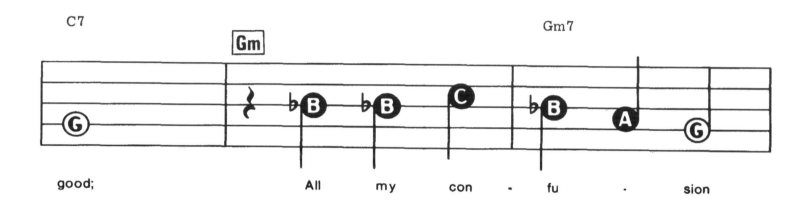

He un - der - stood; All I had to

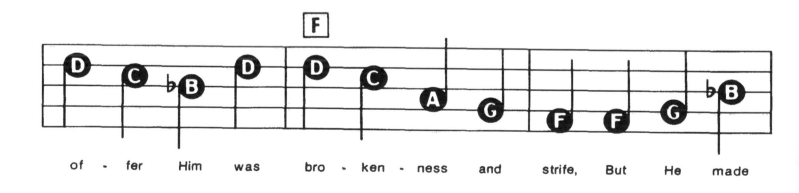

of - fer Him was bro - ken - ness and strife, But He made

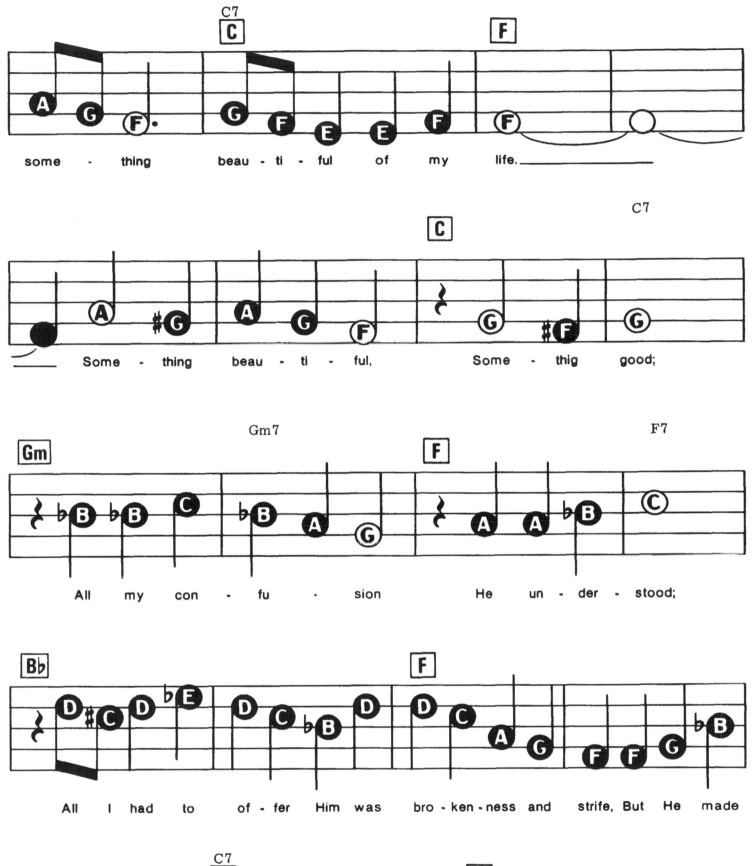

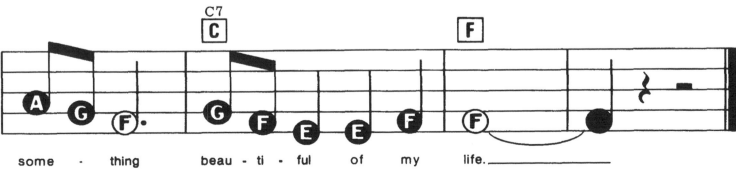

The Spirit Of Jesus Is In This Place

Registration 4
Rhythm: Rock or 8 Beat

Words by William J. & Gloria Gaither
Music by William J. Gaither

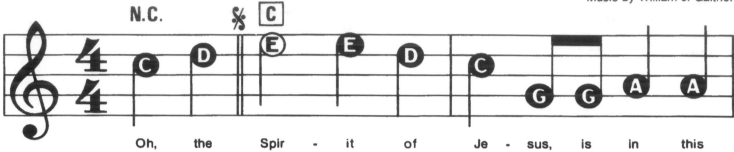

Oh, the Spir - it of Je - sus, is in this

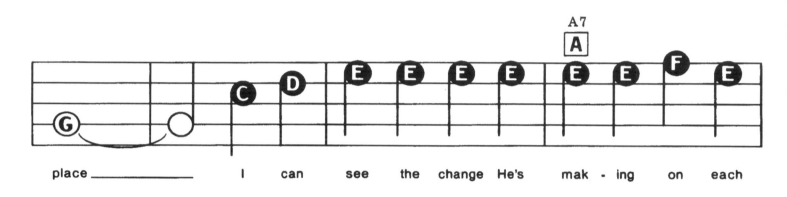

place _____ I can see the change He's mak - ing on each

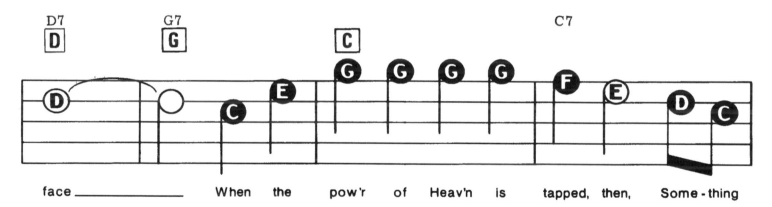

face _____ When the pow'r of Heav'n is tapped, then, Some - thing

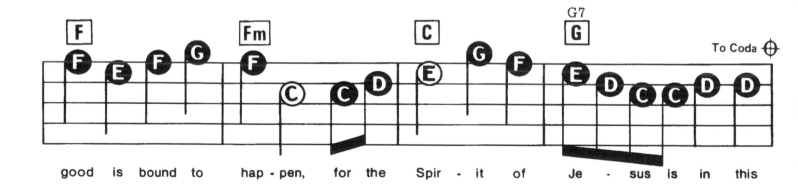

good is bound to hap - pen, for the Spir - it of Je - sus is in this

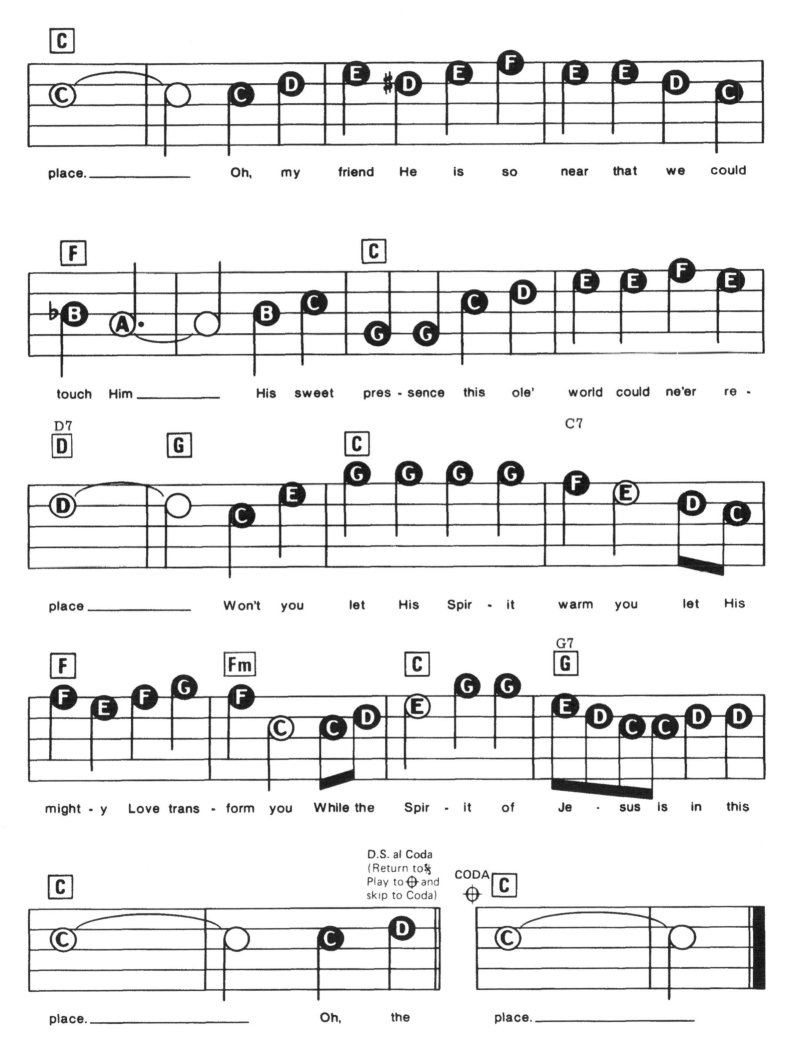

Thanks To Calvary

Registration 2
Rhythm: Rock

Words by William J. & Gloria Gaither
Music by William J. Gaither

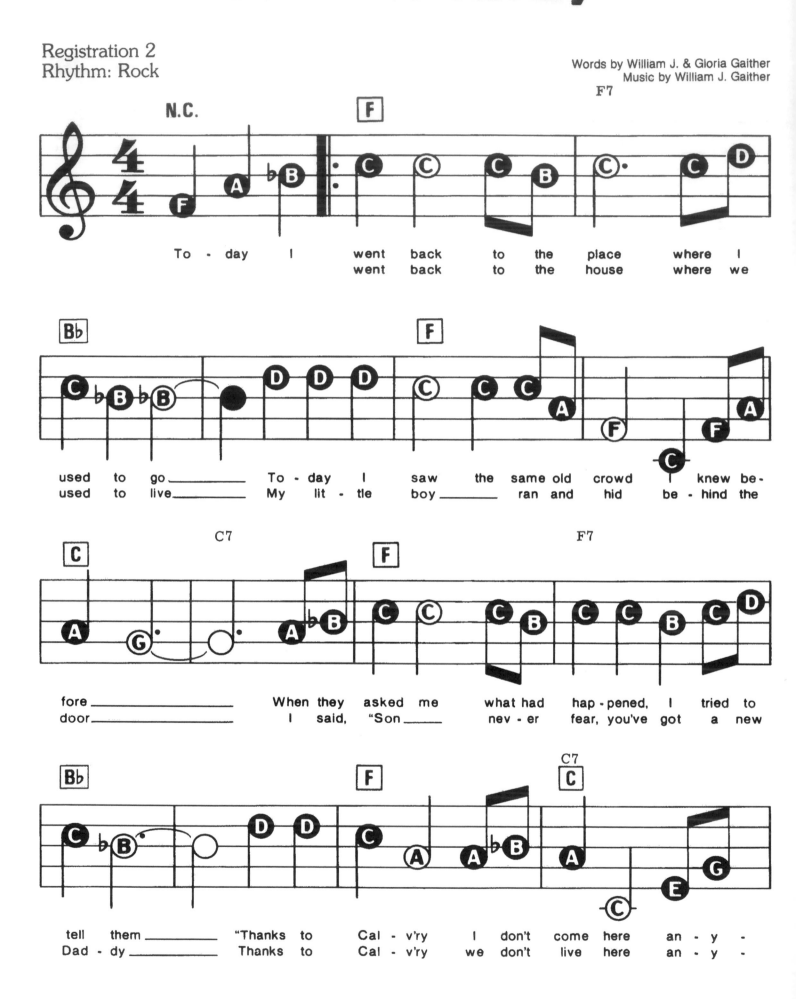

To - day I went back to the place where I
went back to the place house where we

used to go _____ To - day I saw the same old crowd I knew be -
used to live _____ My lit - tle boy _____ ran and hid be - hind the

fore _____ When they asked me what had hap - pened, I tried to
door _____ I said, "Son _____ nev - er fear, you've got a new

tell them _____ "Thanks to Cal - v'ry I don't come here an - y -
Dad - dy _____ Thanks to Cal - v'ry we don't live here an - y -

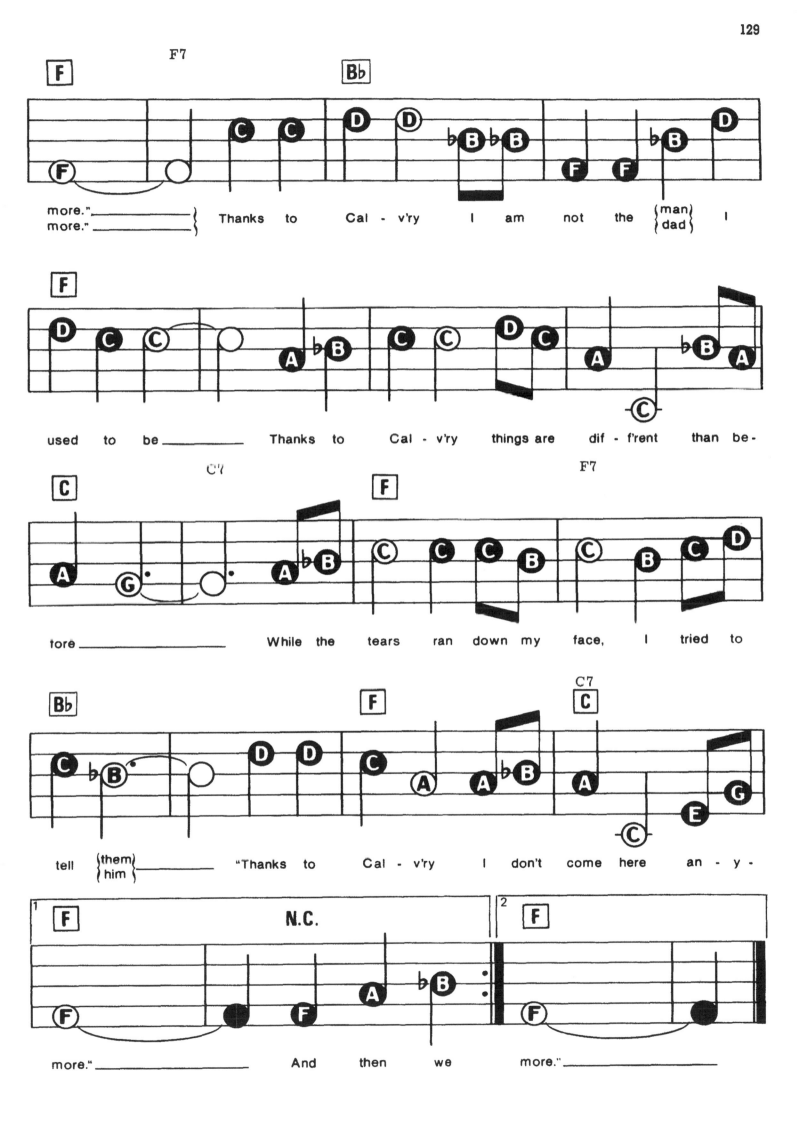

That's What Jesus Means To Me

Registration 3
Rhythm: Ballad or Slow Rock

Words and Music by
William J. Gaither

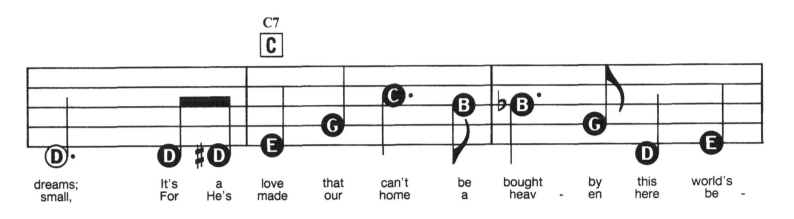

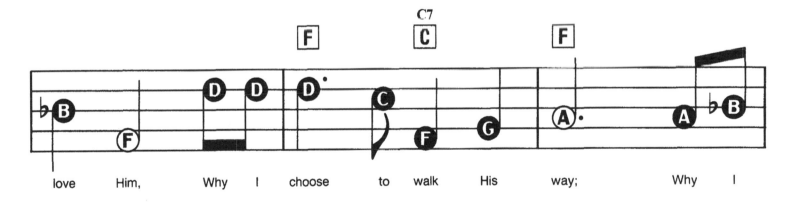

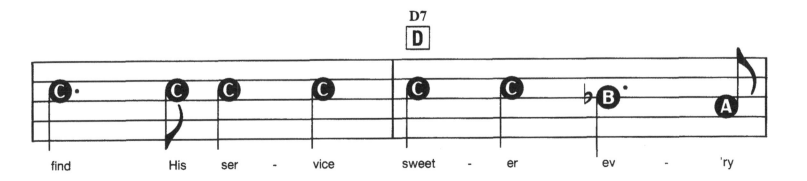

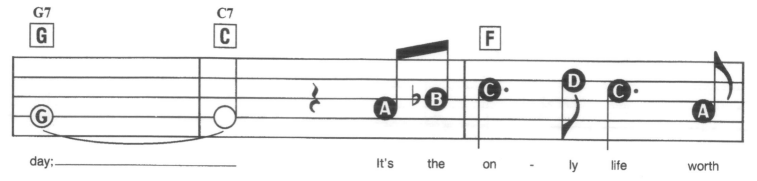

day;_____ It's the on - ly life worth

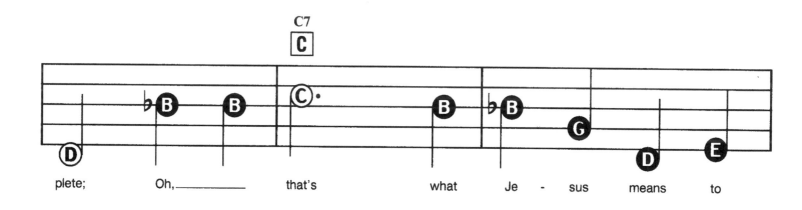

liv - ing He has made my world com - (our home)

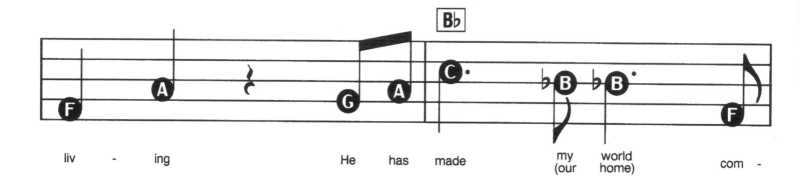

plete; Oh,_____ that's what Je - sus means to

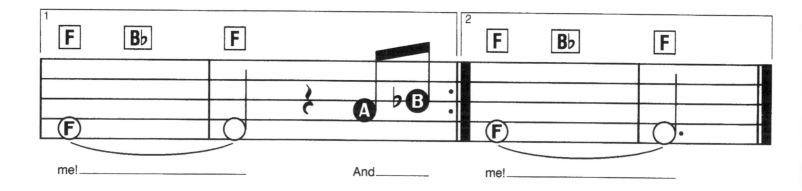

me!_____ And_____ me!

This Is The Day
The Lord Hath Made

Registration 4
Rhythm: Rock

Words by William J. & Gloria Gaither
Music by William J. Gaither

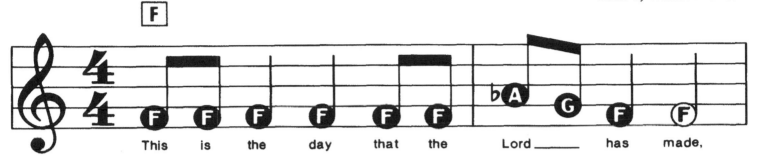

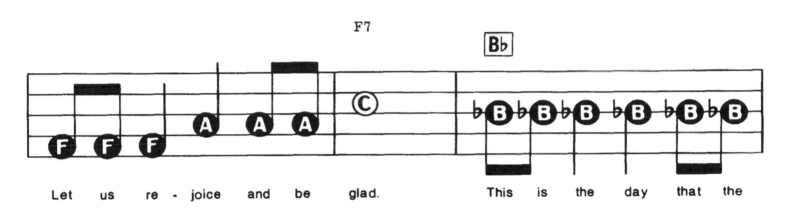

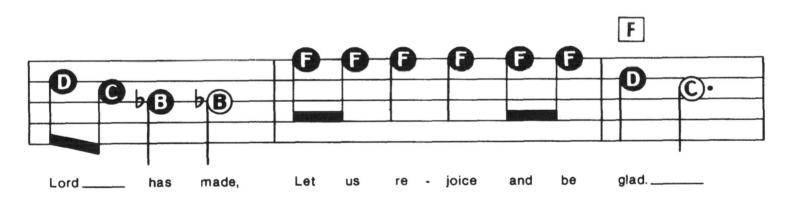

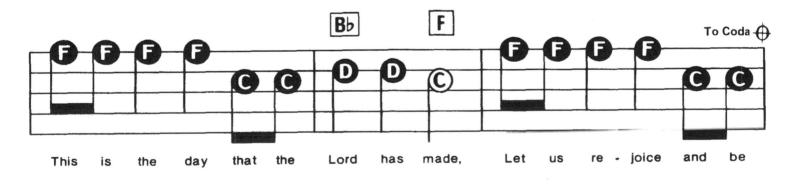

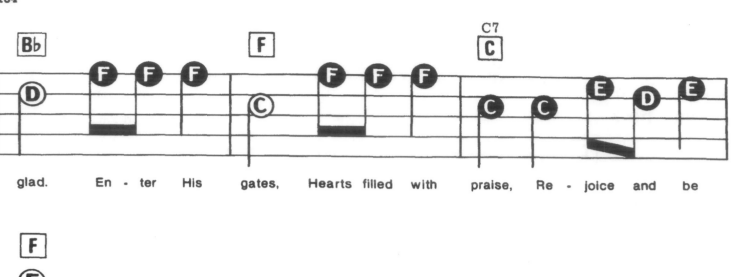

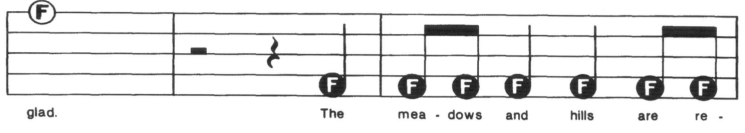

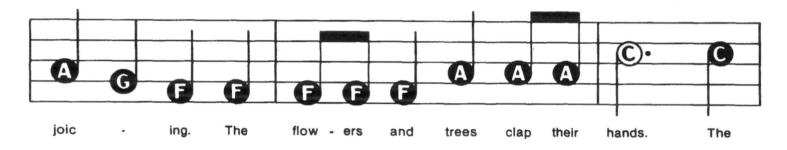

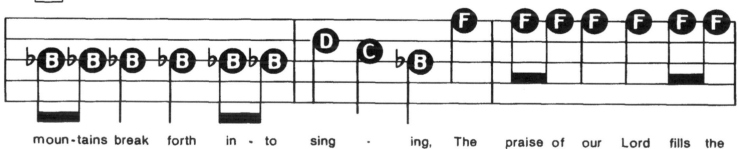

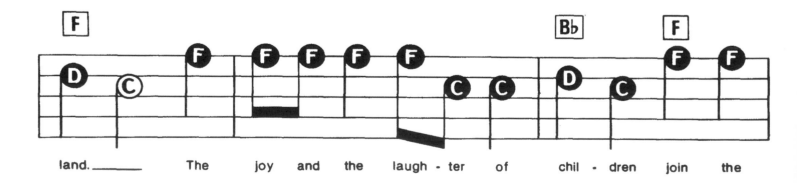

praise of the a - ged and wise. Je - sus is King, Come, join and

sing, Praise fill the sky!

D.C. al Coda
(Return to beginning Play to ⊕ and skip to Coda)

CODA

glad. Now I can see He cares a - bout me. Come, join and

sing Je - sus is King! En - ter His gates Hearts filled with

praise, Re - joice and be glad! _____

There's Something About That Name

Registration 1
Rhythm: Waltz

Words by William J. & Gloria Gaither
Music by William J. Gaither

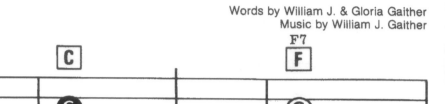

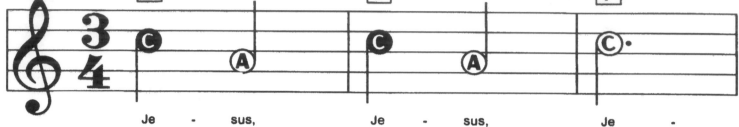

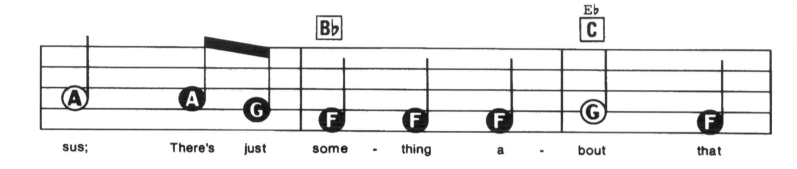

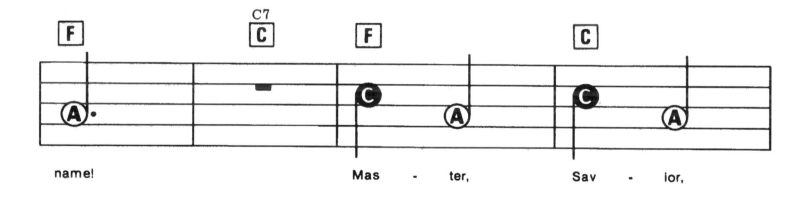

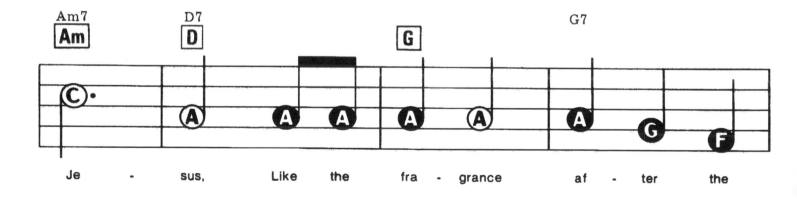

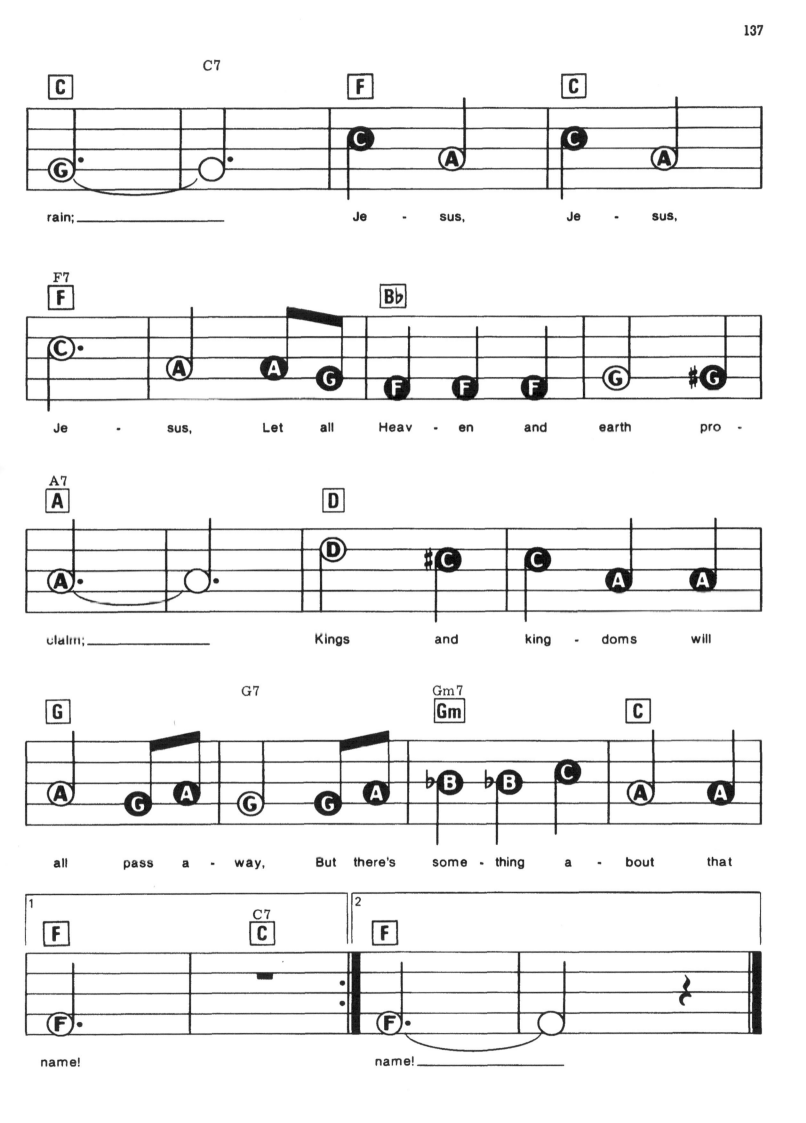

This Could Be The Dawning Of That Day

Registration 2
Rhythm: Swing

Words by William J. & Gloria Gaither
Music by William J. Gaither

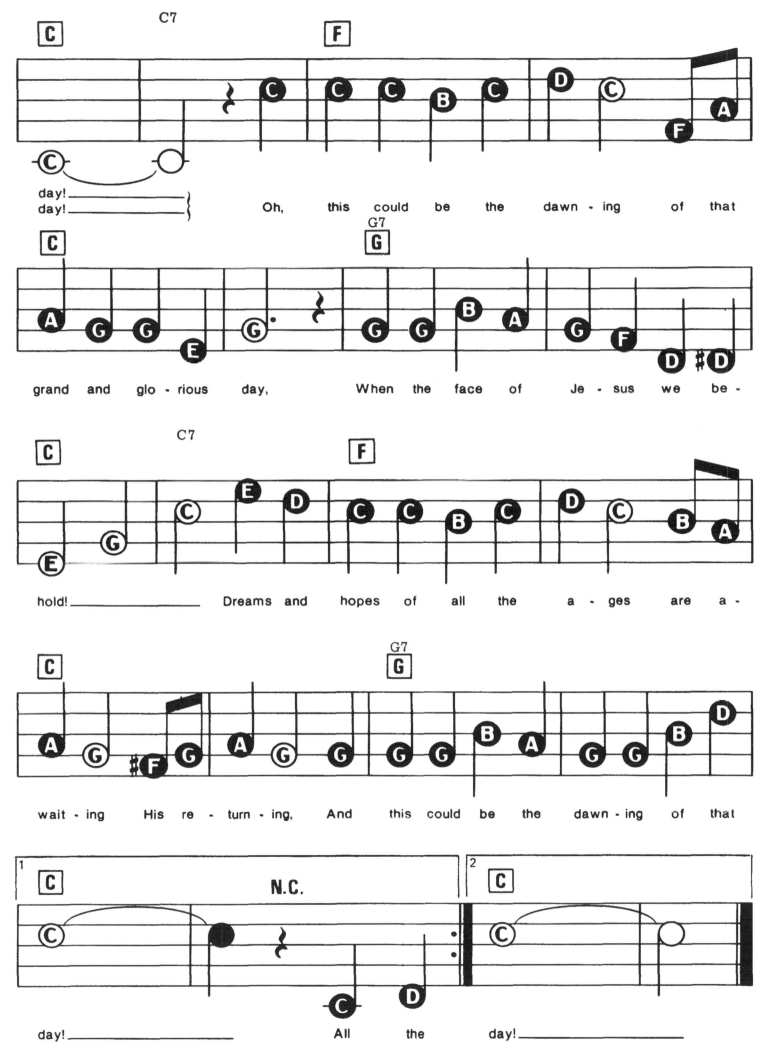

This Is The Time I Must Sing

Registration 5
Rhythm: Waltz

Words by William J. & Gloria Gaither
Music by William J. Gaither

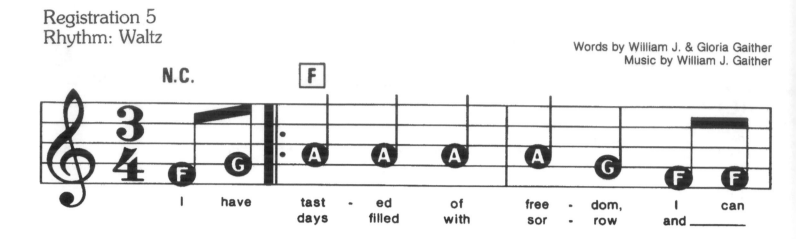

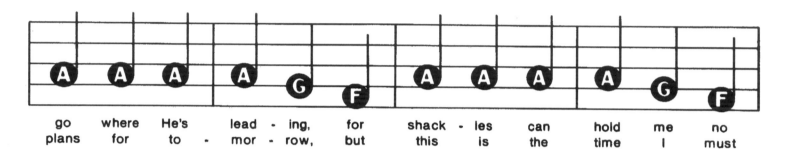

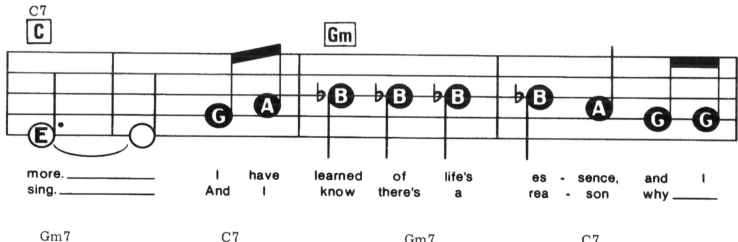

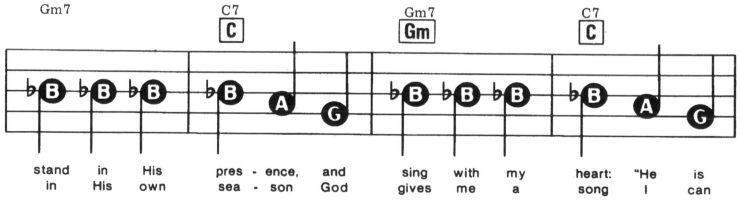

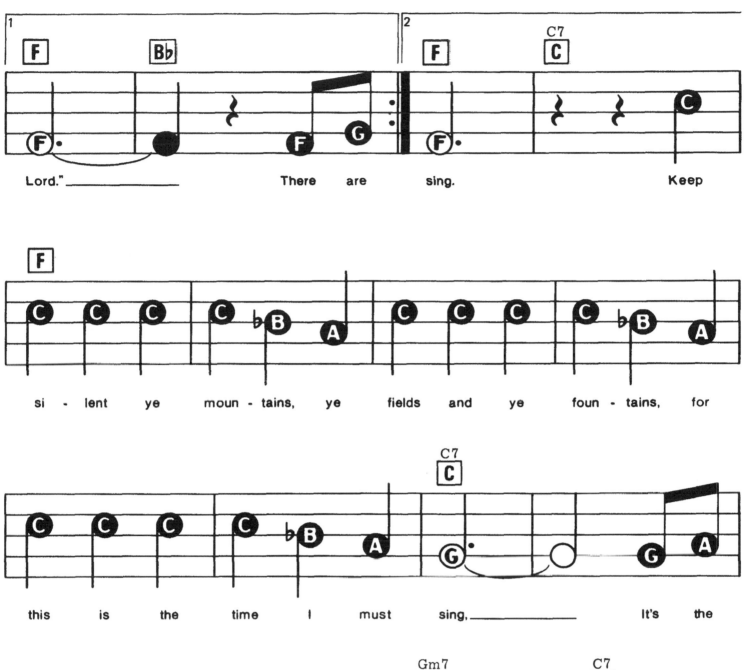

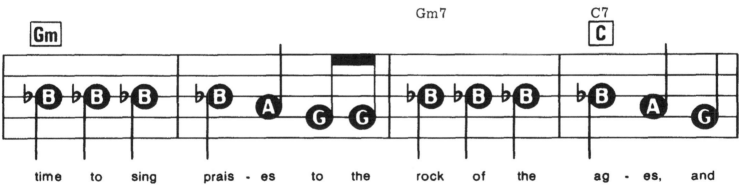

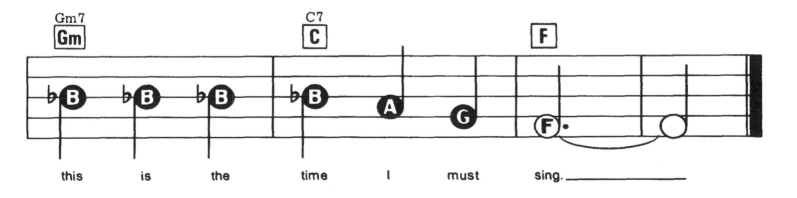

Unshakable Kingdom

Registration 3
Rhythm: Ballad or Slow Rock

By Michael W. Smith, Gloria Gaither,
Bill Gaither

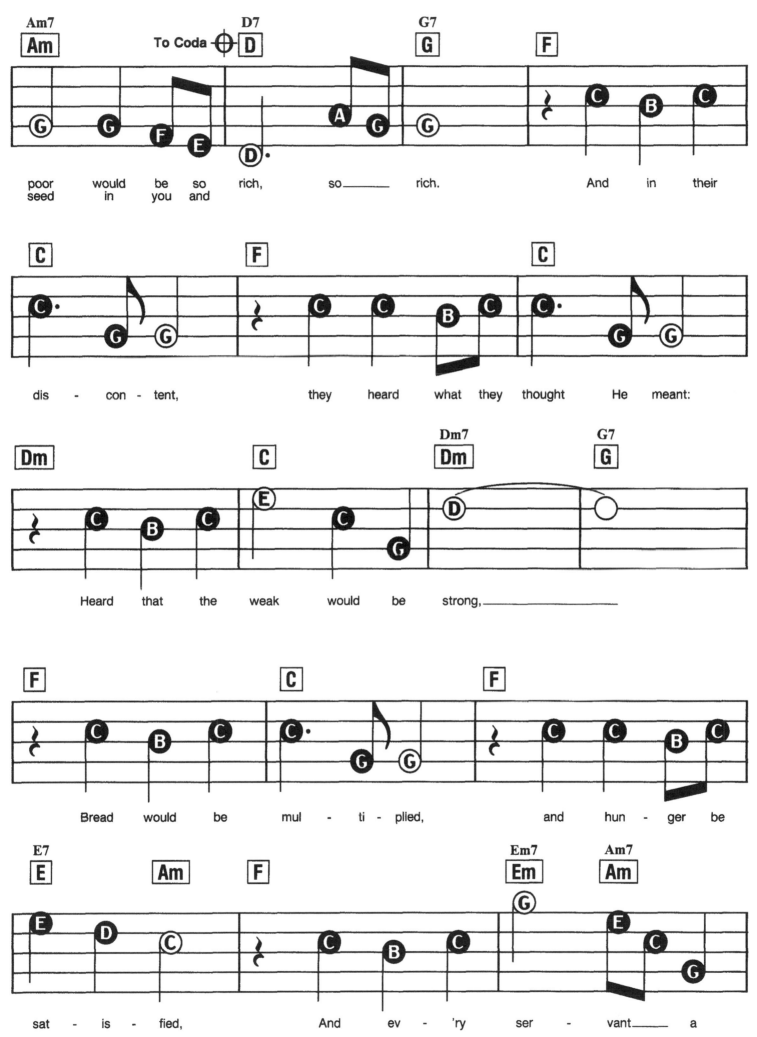

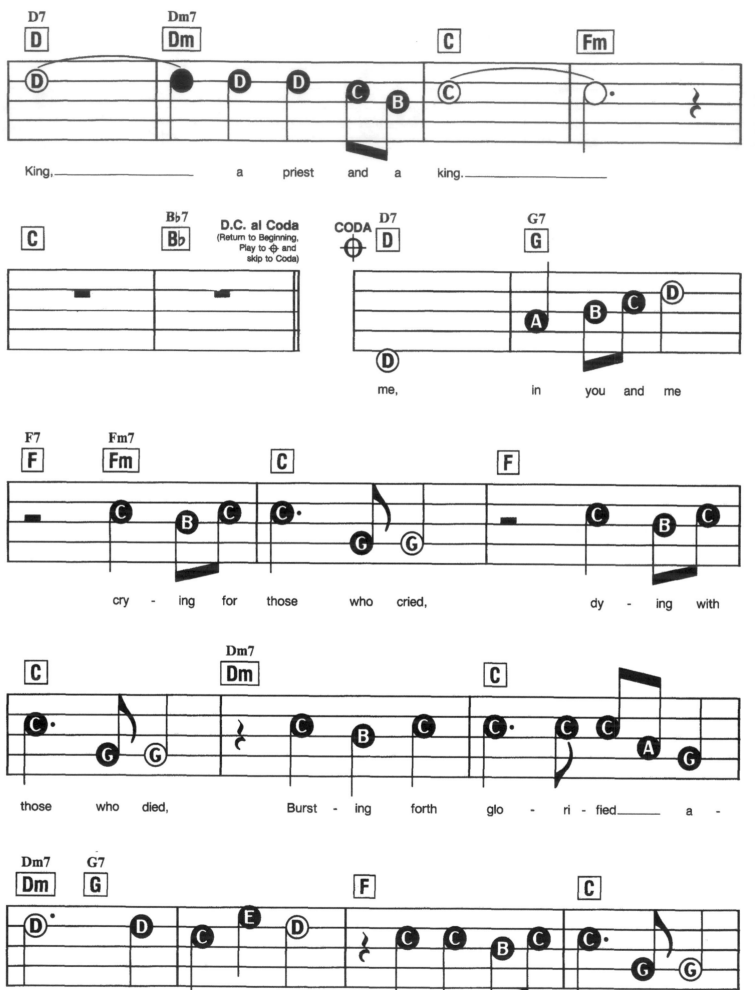

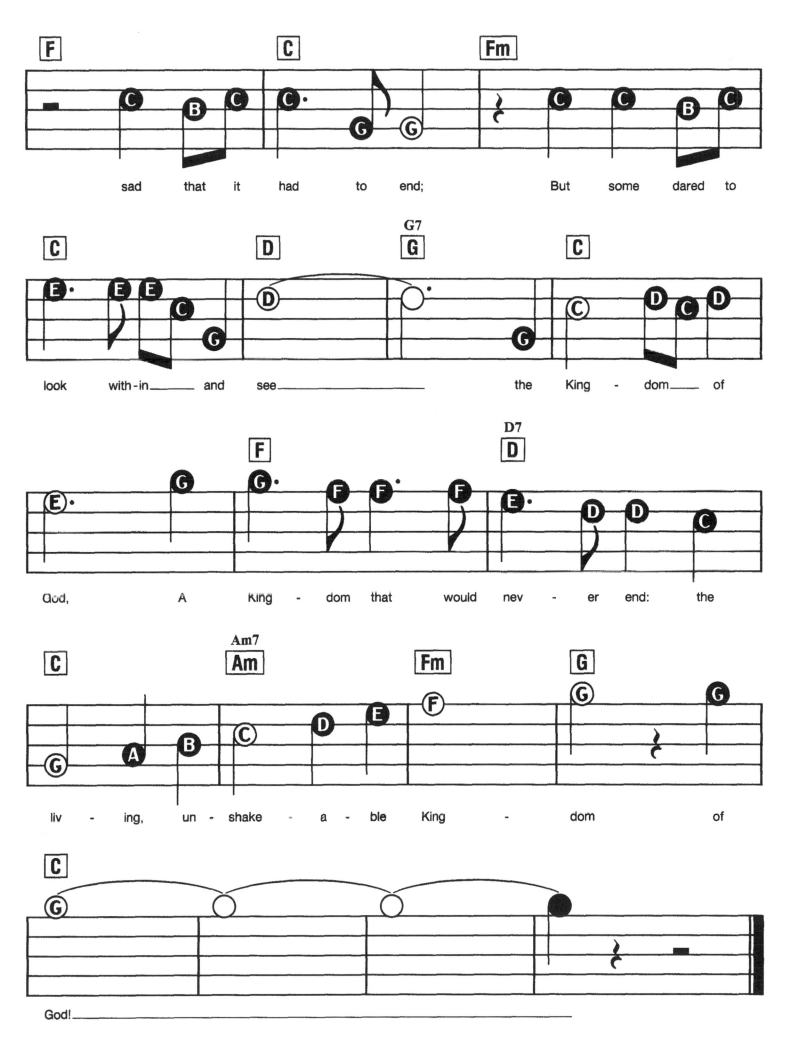

Upon This Rock

Registration 8
Rhythm: Ballad or Slow Rock

Words by Gloria Gaither
Music by Dony McGuire

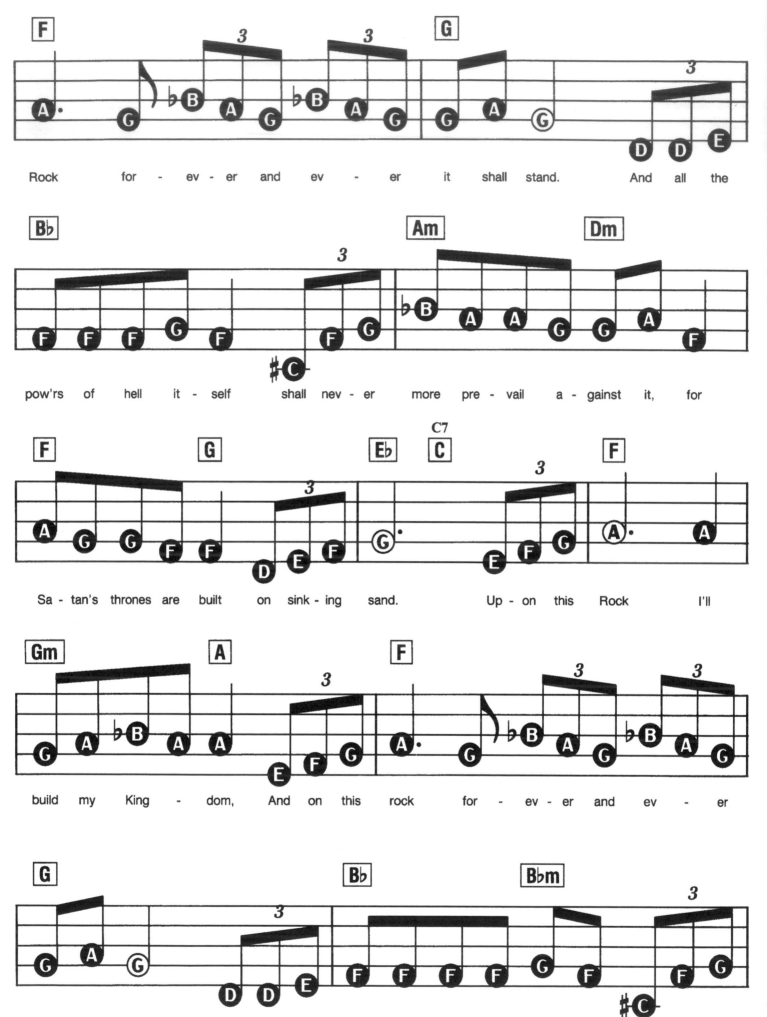

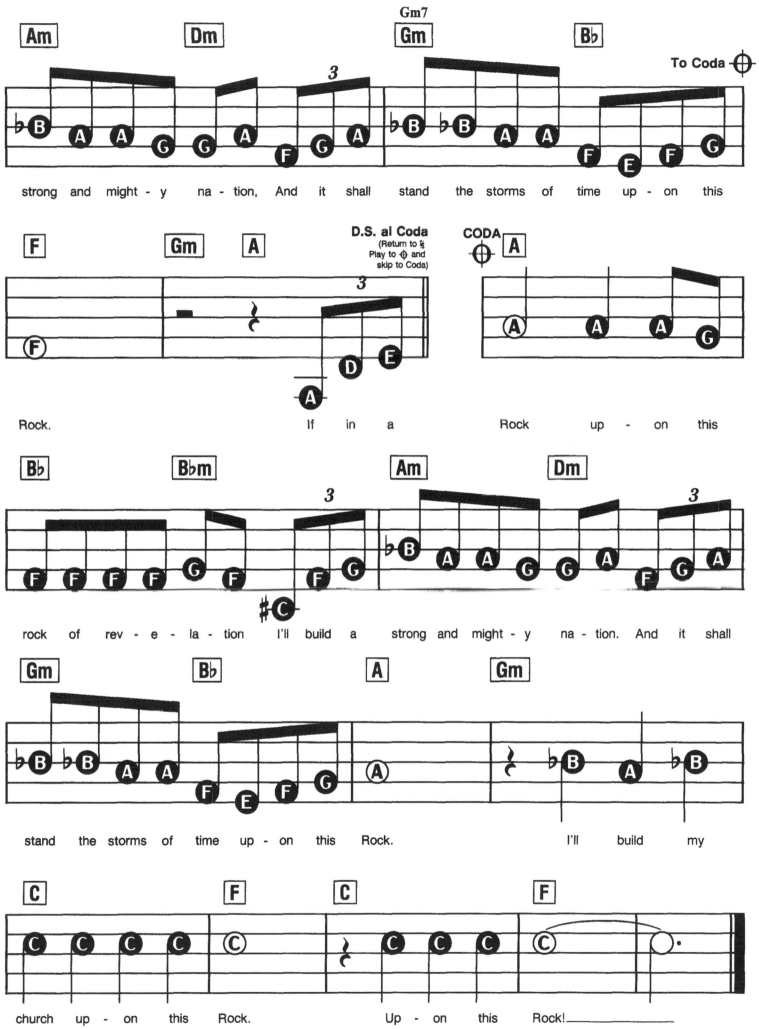

Walk On The Water

Registration 5
Rhythm: Swing

Words by William J. & Gloria Gaither
Music by William J. Gaither

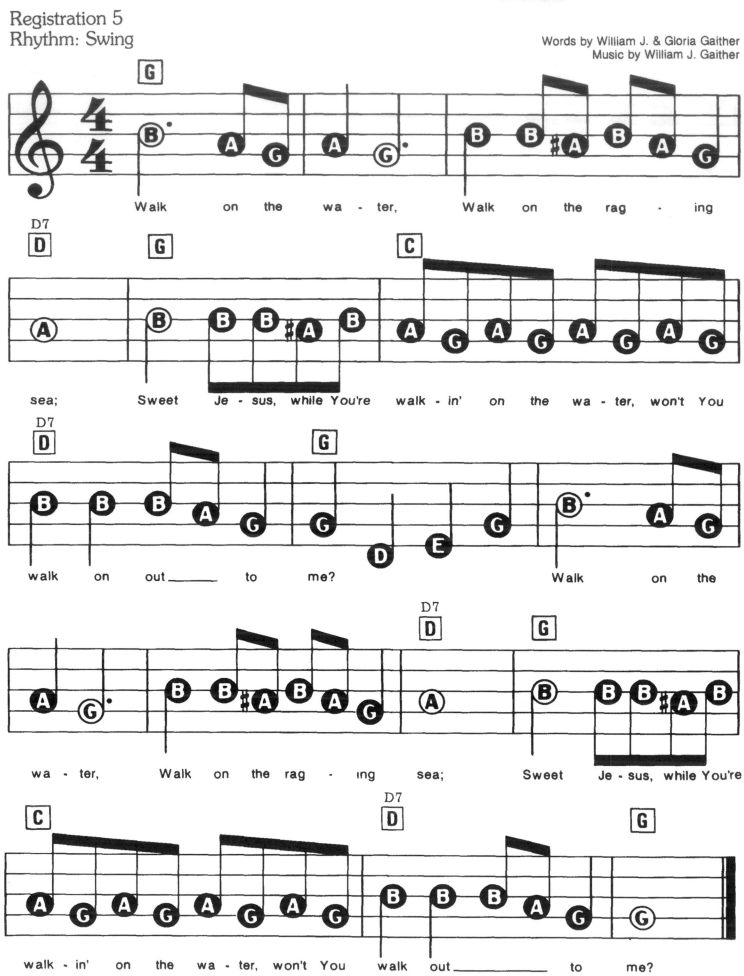

The World Didn't Give It To Me
(And The World Can't Take It Away)

Registration 5
Rhythm: Rock

Words and Music by Gary S. Paxton
and William J. & Gloria Gaither

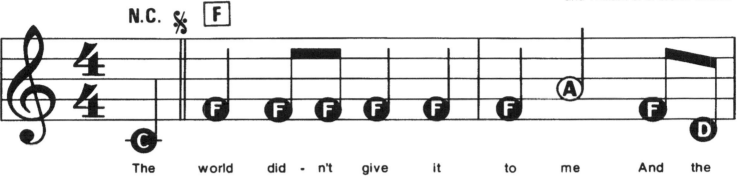

The world did - n't give it to me And the

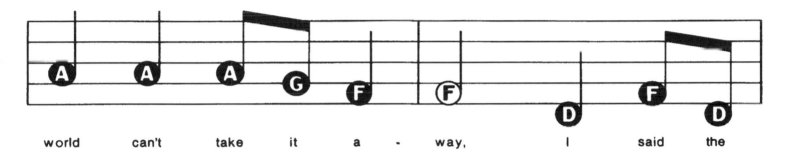

world can't take it a - way, I said the

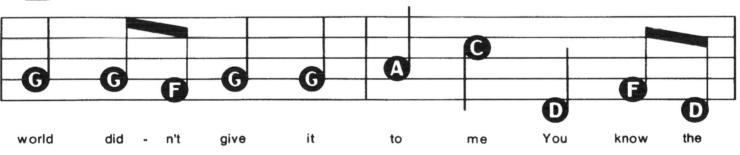

world did - n't give it to me You know the

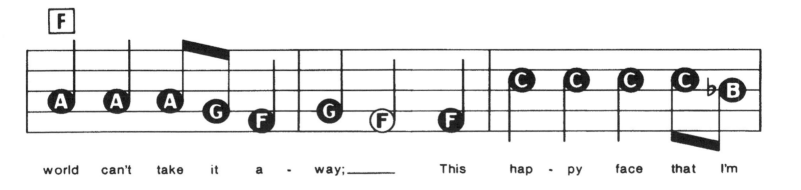

world can't take it a - way;____ This hap - py face that I'm

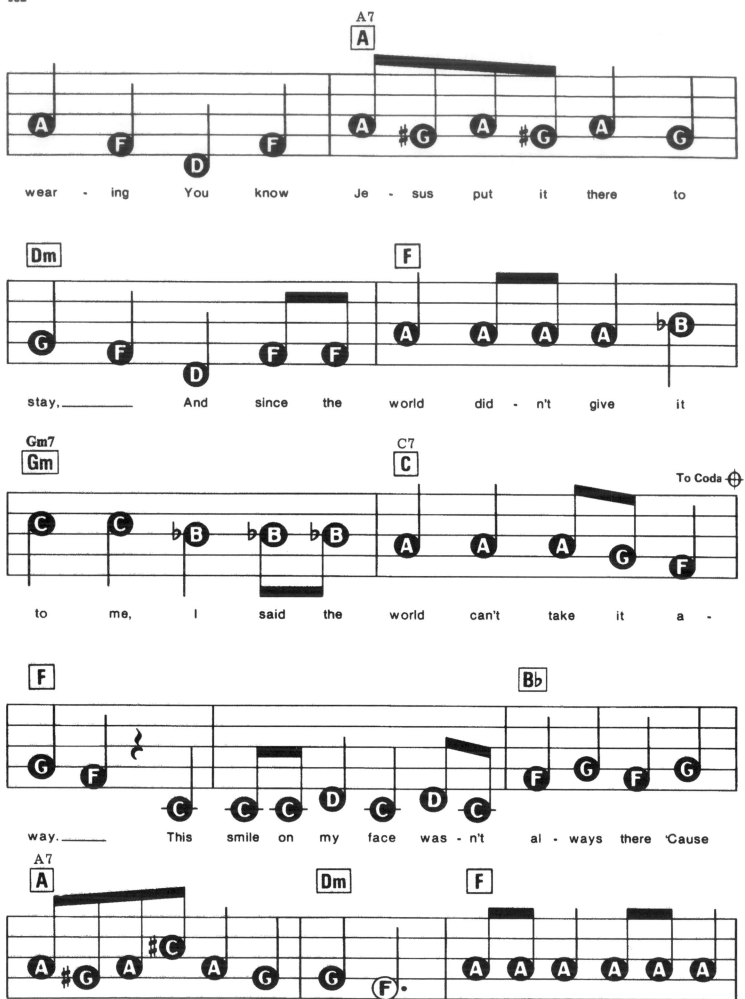

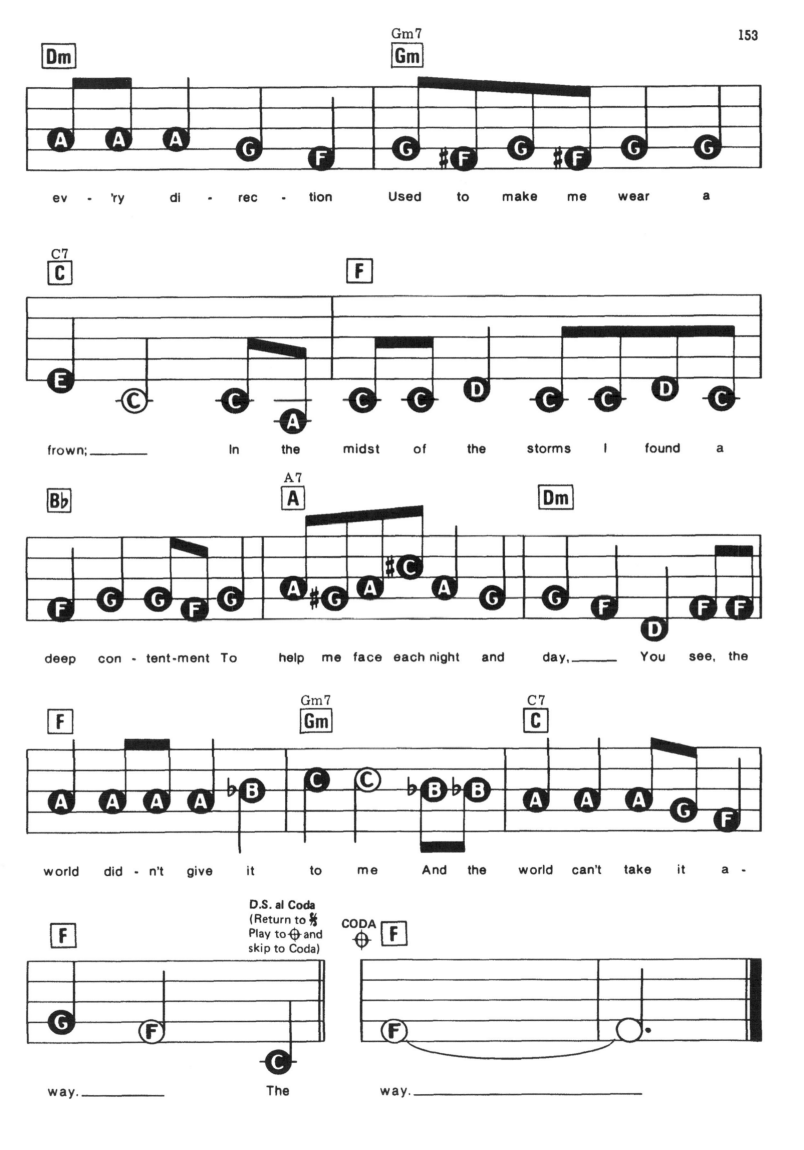

Why Should I Worry Or Fret?

Registration 6
Rhythm: 8 Beat or Pops

Words and Music by
William J. Gaither

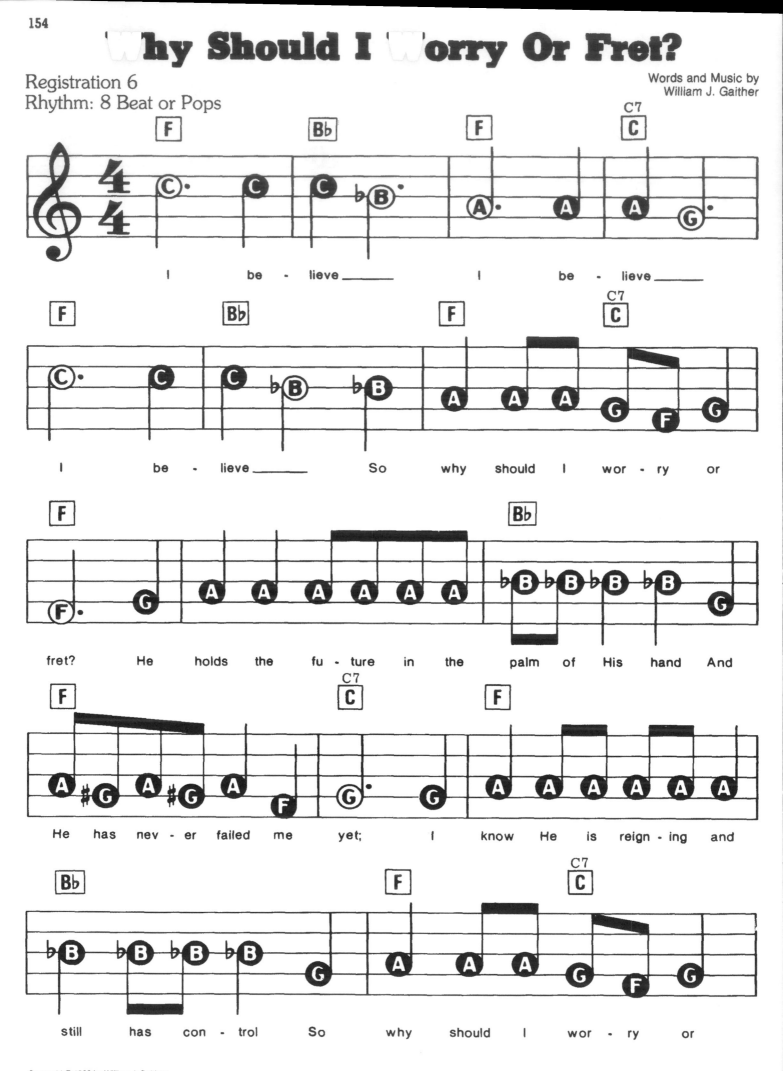

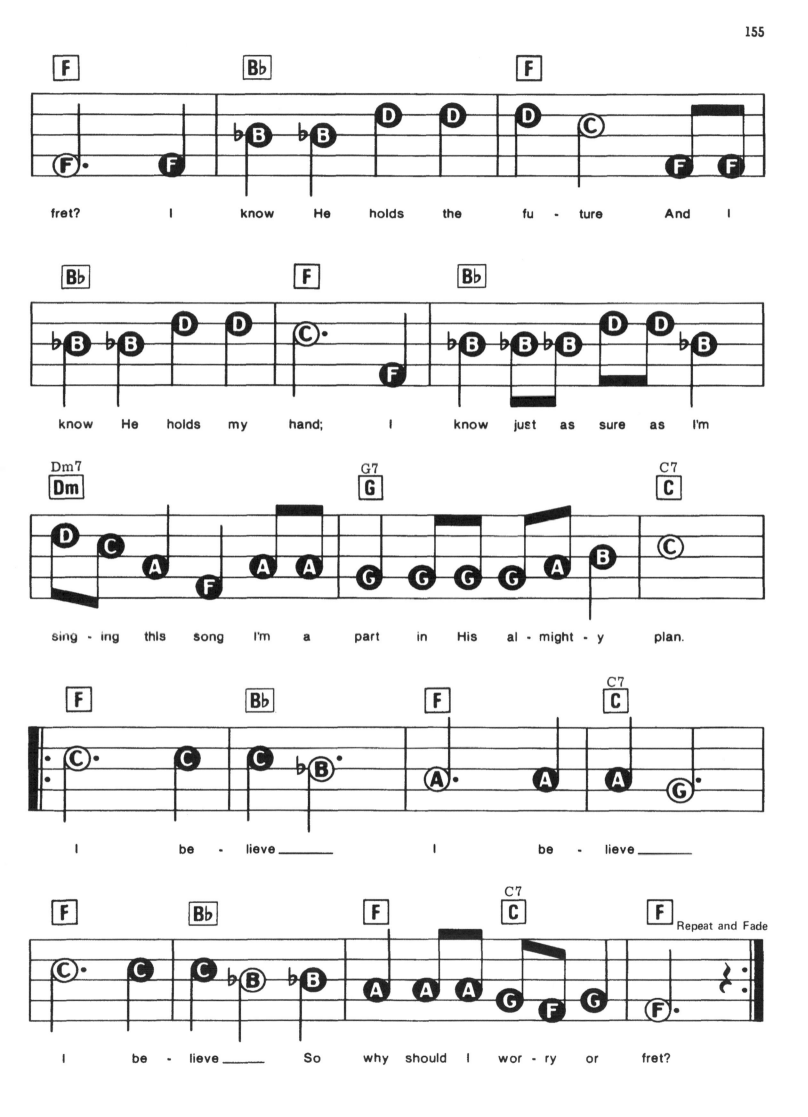

Worthy The Lamb

Registration 2
Rhythm: Waltz

Words by William J. & Gloria Gaither
Music by William J. Gaither

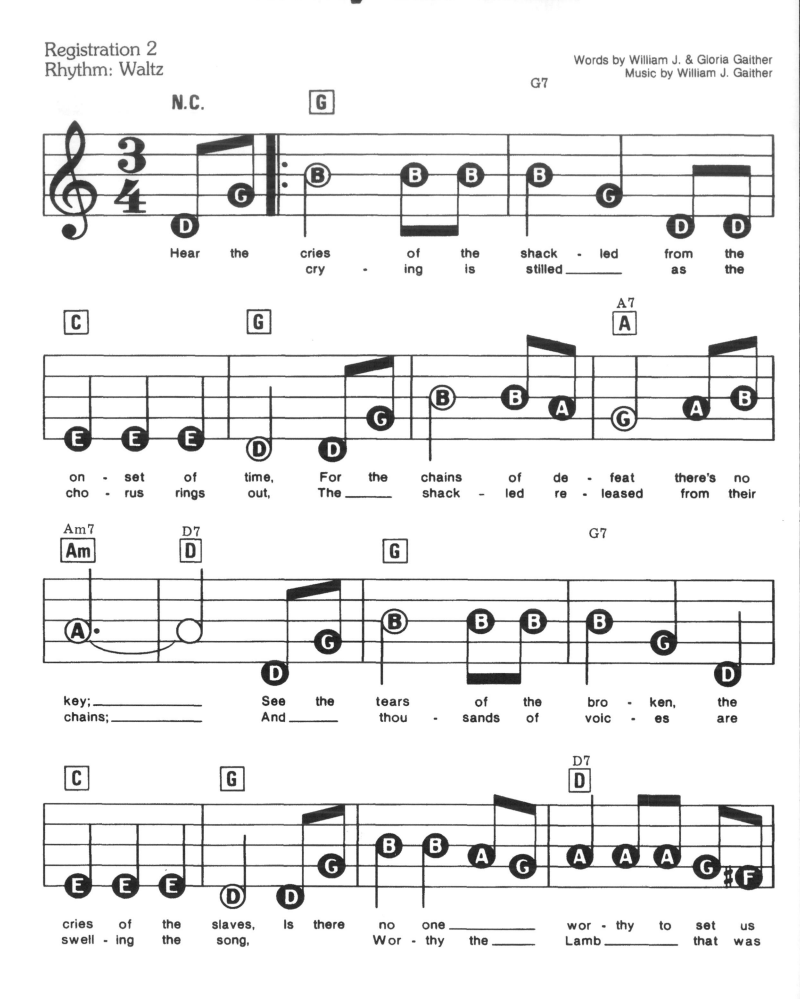

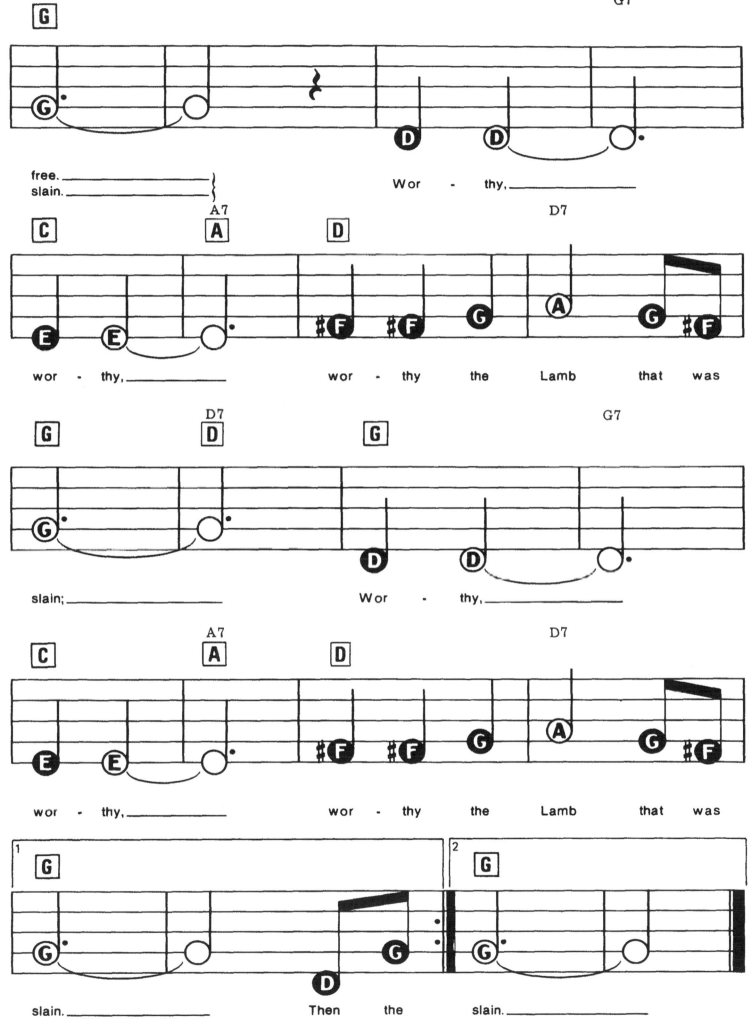

You're Something Special

Registration 1
Rhythm: Waltz

Words by William J. & Gloria Gaither
Music by William J. Gaither

want - ed you to find, so He made you some - thing
want - ed me to find, so He made me some - thing

spec - ial, you're the on - ly one of your kind. My
spec - ial, I'm the on - ly one of my

kind. He made you some - thing spec - ial, He

made you some - thing spec - ial, you're the on - ly

one of your kind.